Not Just
a Game

Not Just a Game
An anthology
of sporting poems

Edited by Andy Croft
and Sue Dymoke

Five Leaves Publications
www.fiveleaves.co.uk

Not Just a Game
(ed.) Andy Croft and Sue Dymoke

Published in 2006 by Five Leaves Publications
PO Box 8786, Nottingham NG1 9AW
www.fiveleaves.co.uk
info@fiveleaves.co.uk

ISBN 1905512139
9781905512133

Five Leaves gratefully acknowledges financial assistance
from Arts Council England

Sporting graphics by Brick (www.brickbats.co.uk)
Designed and typeset by Four Sheets Design & Print Limited
Printed in Nottingham by the Russell Press

Contents

Golf

Hang Gliding

Horse Racing

Motorbike Racing

We Welcome to the Field of Play...

Ian McMillan

It's 1998 and I'm watching Barnsley FC playing Manchester United at Oakwell in the FA Cup after having held them to a draw at Old Trafford. It's one of the most astonishing games I've ever been to, full of the kind of passion and excitement that all matches, all sports, all poems should be full of. The great John Hendrie scores a goal for Barnsley that's so offside a new word should be created to describe how offside it was. It was Ooofside. Then Scott Jones (whatever happened to him?) scores two headed goals and we win 3-2. And in the mayhem and jubilation that follow the final whistle a man leans over to me and says "You won't write a poem about this: you'll write a sonnet!" and that's what this book is about: the sublime meeting of sport and poetry, of movement and skill and an attempt to find a language that can describe and celebrate it properly.

So in this collection you'll find John Arlott, friend of Dylan Thomas and voice of cricket, but also a fine poet in his own right; Ted Hughes writing beautifully about fishing but also about football (You won't write a poem about this, Ted: you'll write a majestic free-verse psalmic incantation!) and UA Fanthorpe creating one of the few decent poems about hang-gliding. There are poems about Brian Clough and Eric Cantona and Brain Lara, and poems about not being picked for the team.

I'm pleased to report, though, that this book isn't just for football fans or cricket lovers or hang-gliding anoraks. There are poems here on netball, highland games, polo, ping-pong, canoeing, rock climbing, and loads more, all jostling for our attention at the side of the pitch/green/pool/court/hang-gliding arena.

Now I don't want to suggest that this book is simply for lovers of sport, the people who turn to the back pages before the book reviews, who flick on Sky Sports before they go anywhere near BBC 4. This book is for people who love poetry as much as (or more than) they love sport, and it's for people who have no interest in sport; because the crucial thing to say about sporting poems is that they are about human endeavour, about hopes and fears, and about how we construct ways of living with each other and with ourselves.

Historically sport and poetry are linked, of course: in the early Olympics verse speaking was something that people did alongside athletics. You could get a garland for a great poem in the same way that you could get a garland for running a mile. Early oral poetry would often celebrate feats of strength and daring, and contemporary oral poetry can be heard from the football terraces every week, not only celebrating feats of strength and daring, but questioning the referee's parentage and posing knotty and indeed intractable philosophical questions about the sexual orientation of the goalkeeper. In the broadsheets and the fanzines and the message boards and the blogs the poetry continues in explosions of language that often reaches hang-gliding heights in attempts to describe the difficult-to-describe. At Oakwell the other day, one of the opposition defenders had a huge thatch of red hair. As he came near us to take a throw in, a man in front of me shouted "You look like a busted cushion!" Poetry!

Enjoy this book. The whistle is about to blow to start the game. The crowd are waiting, raising their voices and clapping their hands. The teams are ready, or the lone sportsperson is preparing to move. The poem is waiting to start, like a greyhound in the traps. Or a swimmer on a board. Or a hang-glider at the top of a hill...

Introduction

"For what do we live, but to make sport..."
JANE AUSTEN

Poetry and sport have always run along well together. The original Greek Games had their origins over two thousand years ago in poetic and musical competition. The lyric poet Pindar is renowned for his poems celebrating the victories of athletes in the great games at Olympia, Delphi, Corinth and Nemea. The first marathon runner, Phidippides, is celebrated in Herodotus. Homer spent an entire book of *The Odyssey* describing the Phaeacian games. Shelley, Wordsworth, Keats and Coleridge wrote poems about climbing; Byron and Swinburne celebrated swimming in verse; Morris and Houseman wrote poems about running; Blake, Carroll and Conan Doyle wrote about cricket; Crabbe, Goldsmith and Clare about village-green sports.

The modern Olympics included medals for poetry as late as 1948 and number of internationally-known poets have kept alive the tradition of praising athletic achievement — for example, William Carlos Williams's 'At the Ball Game', Wole Soyinka's 'Muhammad Ali at the Ringside, 1985', Kenneth Koch's 'Ko, or a Season on Earth', Marianne Moore's 'Baseball and Writing', Lorca's 'Lament for Ignacio Sanchez Mejias' and Nicholas Guillen's 'Small Ode to a Black Cuban Boxer'.

However for some twentieth century writers closer to home, poetry and sport seemed to inhabit wholly different worlds. Yeats, for example, dismissed those who 'run hither and thither in some foolish sport' while Kipling characterised the English as a decadent people who had 'contented their souls/With the flannelled fools at the wicket or the muddied oafs at the goals.' The image of poetry as a private and personal act of reflection appeared to be at odds with the shared, public and physical passions of sport. For a while, writing about sport was left to the track-side and touch-line hyperbole of commentators and the studio and back-page cliché of 'poetry in motion'. Poetry about sport seemed to disappear underground — into light verse, *Wisden*, match-day programmes, fanzines, terraces songs. In recent years however there has been a resurgence in sports poetry — one website dedicated to poems about football currently hosts over 7,000 poems. Aspects of sport have become potential topics for a much wider range of poets who explore issues about family, childhood, identity, class, culture and relationships in their writing. Some use humour, others have a keen ear for the absurd or an eye for the extraordinary detail.

Although there have been a number of sport-specific anthologies in the last fifteen years, like Ian Horn (ed.) *Verses United* (1993) and Alan Ross (ed.) *The Kingswood Book of Cricket* (1992), *Not Just a Game* is the first general anthology of poems about sport since Alan Bold's *The Poetry of Motion* (1986) and Vernon Scannell's *Sporting Literature* (1987), both long out of print. Any anthology of poems says a good deal about the character of the society that produced it. For much of the twentieth-century, poems were published by men whose tastes in both sport and poetry were shaped by their class and education. We could have filled this book with memoir-poems about playing cricket, or post-Nick Hornby poems about watching football. Of course we have selected some of these but we have tried to cast our net more widely, to represent an age which has produced athletes like Denise Lewis, Kelly Holmes and Paula Radcliffe, in which female golfers are making the cut, Asian boxers and Scottish curlers capture spectators' imaginations and cricket players of both sexes can share in the joy of their Ashes' victories. We have endeavoured to move beyond the mainstream and feature an extensive range of sports, including canoeing, netball, skating and climbing, as well as less athletic but no less skillful sports like bowls, darts, fishing and pool. We have not included any poems about fox-hunting, which does not seem to us to be a sport at all. As Cowper wrote, it is a strange kind of game, 'That owes its pleasures to another's pain'.

As many of the poems in this collection demonstrate, poems about sport often carry other subjects with them. (In South Africa and New Zealand in the 1980s, poetry about rugby played a highly public role in the struggles against Apartheid.) Poems about cricket, for example, are invariably also about masculinity and England, or at least a particular idea of Englishness. In Sir Henry Newbolt's 1897 poem '*Vitai Lampada*', ideas of youth, class, manhood, education, national identity and imperial destiny are all located in a game of public-school cricket ('Play up! play up! and play the game!'). In the twenty-first century, poets do not always sing the praises of the *victor ludorum*. They are often more interested in questioning male and female values, considering not just competitiveness, but also pain and pleasure, shared experience and isolation, exploring the sociology, the rituals and language of sport.

Sport is now a global and mass phenomenon. Few people in contemporary Britain are able to exempt themselves from its pull whether as participants, spectators or supporters. Poetry too, is a mass phenomenon. Many people write poetry at some time in their lives. Not everyone who runs onto the pitch expects to play in the World Cup final. Not everyone who picks up a pen thinks they will win the Nobel Prize for Literature. Sport and poetry are both democratic activities. Anyone can join in.

To play sport, as to watch it, requires an affirmation of our common humanity. Whether you are in the crowd or on the pitch, sport offers a shared sense of success and failure, a knowledge of humility and an apprehension of beauty. Individual achievement and collective effort, personal satisfaction and public pride, superhuman endurance and skill exchanged for sheer enjoyment or perhaps immortality — if this isn't the stuff of poetry, we don't know what is. *Not Just a Game* captures the tension and the laughter, the pain and the pleasure, and the blood, sweat and tears. This is not just a book for sports fans. This is not just a book for poetry lovers.

It's not just a game.

Andy Croft and Sue Dymoke
May 2006

Selima Hill

My Happiest Day

My happiest day was not my wedding day.
My happiest day
was the day we all played baseball
after exams were over
out on the baseball pitch,
I had been lying all night
with encyclopaedias piled on top of me
"to strengthen my limbs"
and I had come out onto the pitch
in the immaculate Jerusalem-white clothes
I had spent all morning
cleaning and pressing and peeling on and off,
and when the ball came sailing out of the clouds
towards my hands
I was the one who caught it —
my hands,
like laps,
or home,
barely touching its belly
as I guided it out of the sky.
Mother Maria yelled *Catch*
and I caught it every time.
So what's so great about catching a baseball ball?
What's the use of being so happy then?
I've got to concentrate on catching everything
you and the world and its wives
and various pungent mistresses
care to throw at me now,
aged fifty-one.
And Mother Maria's got nothing to do with it.
She probably never even touched a man.

11

Camilla Doyle

A Game of Bowls
(written during an air raid)

My body's crouched beneath a "Table Shelter",
  But my unhampered mind is far away;
My hands may quiver and my breathing falter
  But still my memory watches men at play;
They played at bowls — I see the "woods" still rolling,
  And hear the gentle clinking when they touch;
I see the friendly smiles that greet good bowling;
  My shelter shakes, but I shan't mind too much
If only I can keep those bowlers playing
  Just as they played last month, beside a wall
Of sunlit yellow stone — yes, they are staying;
  I hear soft chimes, I hear a ring dove call,
And all the pleasure of the men who played
  Reaches me still and keeps me unafraid.

Pauline Stainer

The Bowls Match

Being short-sighted,
she had trusted
the opthalmic surgeon
to refocus light with the knife;
cut close
to the visual axis,
alter the curvature of the cornea
with a diamond-tipped scalpel.

Looking up,
she saw the sun through the glass,
and beyond the hospital hedge
ladies on the lawn
playing bowls
in crisp hats and light summer clothes,
hands raised above their heads
to clap a victory.

Their applause
for unerring alignment
was silent through the pane;
and they should have worn
changeable silks
for her perfected vision —

but she saw them
as if from a clerestory,
stout and middle-aged
in the undeceiving distance,
arms upheld in hierarchy,
radiant figures
at the scene
of an unidentified miracle.

George Jowett

from *Blow by Blow*

I'm not the first by any means to share
A love of boxing and of poetry.
No, boxer/writers are by no means rare,
I share a long, illustrious ancestry
— George Bernard Shaw, Gene Tunney and Lord B
To name a few. In the modern annal,
The one we're still compiling currently,
The prime example must be Vernon Scannell,
Ex-pug and fine poet. (And that's not just flannel.)

I'm not like him. I never was a pro.
I boxed at school but wasn't good enough
To make a go of it. Modest? Hell, no,
Though by our peers we were considered tough,
The truth is we weren't made of sterner stuff
At all. And if perhaps you're wondering why
I took it up, the art of fisticuffs,
I'll tell you. In winter we kept warm and dry
Inside the school gymnasium. A boy could die

Cross-country running out on Hampstead Heath,
Or playing soccer in the wind and rain.
Who wants a runny nose and chattering teeth?
For outdoor sports you had to be insane.
Far better box. A boy must use his brain.
Besides, like Martin Luther King, I had a dream,
A family tradition to maintain.
My brothers both had led the boxing team
And so must I, I thought. (How foolish now they seem

The ambitions of our youth.) Still, they explain
Why I began to box. I loved it too
And didn't mind the bruises or the pain
When some kid's long left hand came snaking through
My guard. I wore those bruises, black and blue,
Like campaign medals with a soldier's pride.
Silly? I know it is, and yet it's true,
Boxing somehow made me feel good inside.
Though why that should be so, like you, I'm mystified.

All this, of course, was thirty years ago.
I haven't laced the gloves on since that time;
At least, unlike George Foreman, though, I know
(How can I put it?) that I'm past my prime,
Well past it. I'll admit the fact that I'm
Not young or fit enough to fight. OK?
(You'd think that growing older was a crime.
It takes a brave man nowadays to say
"That's it. I quit. Time to admit, I've had my day.")

I'm still a fight fan. In the cheaper seats
At shows throughout the North I can be found.
For sheer excitement I've found nothing beats
A grandstand finish in the final round
As two men slug it out. Then, at the sound
Of the bell, instantly the action ends
And grinning hugely, with their arms around
Each other, former foes become firm friends.
It's funny how cathartic a good punch-up tends

To be. Yes, purged of all hostility,
It leaves us cleansed and calm, our faith restored
In man and his innate nobility.
At times I have been moved, yes, even awed
By what I've seen. And could I but record
The heroism I have seen displayed
In the ring, my work's success would be assured.
If I could get it down I'd have it made.
Unfortunately it's not that easy I'm afraid.

Still, even so, when I began to seek
A subject I could write about in verse,
A subject with the right sort of mystique,
I turned to boxing. Yes, I could do worse
I thought than chronicle the sad reverse
In Ali's fortunes. Poor old Muhammad,
The first to earn a million dollar purse,
Now paying dearly for the fights he had.
I had a working title too — the Aliad.

But no, that's not my story, I decided,
For Ali has been hymned by better men.
Bud Schulberg, José Torrés have provided
Far better tributes than my ball point pen
Could manage. No, I had to think again.
Some local hero who has been neglected
And overlooked till now. But who? And then,
Suddenly inspired, I recollected
Brian Graham. The perfect choice I reflected.

The more I mused the more I was convinced
That Brian's story was the one for me.
A short and simple tale, yet it evinced
All that is best in us, as you shall see.
And unlike Rocky I or II or III,
It's true. I swear it is, yes, every word,
Packed with pathos, rich in humanity.
So let me tell you simply what occurred,
A tale the like of which I doubt you've ever heard...

16

Vernon Scannell

from *First Fight*

Bite on gumshield,
Guard held high,
The crowd are silenced,
All sounds die.
Lead with the left,
Again, again;
Watch for the opening,
Feint and then
Hook to the body
But he's blocked it and
Slammed you back
With a fierce right hand.
Hang on grimly,
The fog will clear,
Sweat in your nostrils,
Grease and fear.
You're hurt and staggering,
Shocked to know
That the story's altered:
He's the hero!

But the mist is clearing,
The referee snaps
A rapid warning
And he smartly taps
Your hugging elbow
And then you step back
Ready to counter
The next attack,
But the first round finishes
Without mishap.

You suck in the air
From the towel's skilled flap.
A voice speaks urgently
Close to your ear:
"Keep your left going, boy,
Stop him getting near.
He wants to get close to you,
So jab him off hard;
When he tries to slip below,
Never mind your guard,
Crack him with a solid right,
Hit him on the chin,
A couple downstairs
And then he'll pack it in."

Slip in the gumshield
Bite on it hard,
Keep him off with your left,
Never drop your guard.
Try a left hook,
But he crosses with a right
Smack on your jaw
And Guy Fawkes Night
Flashes and dazzles
Inside your skull,
Your knees go bandy
And you almost fall.
Keep the left jabbing,
Move around the ring,
Don't let him catch you with
Another hook or swing.
Keep your left working,
Keep it up high,
Stab it out straight and hard,
Again — above the eye.
Sweat in the nostrils,
But nothing now of fear.

Vernon Scannell

Mastering the Craft

To make the big time you must learn
The basic moves; left jab and hook,
The fast one-two, right-cross; the block
And counter-punch; the way to turn
Opponents on the ropes; the feint
To head or body; uppercut;
To move inside the swing and set
Your man up for the kill. But don't
Think that this is all; a mere
Beginning only. It is through
Fighting often you will grow
Accomplished in manoeuvres more
Subtle than the textbooks know:
How to change your style to meet
The unexpected move that might
Leave you open to the blow
That puts the lights out for the night.

The same with poets: they must train,
Practise metre's footwork, learn
The old iambic left and right,
To change the pace and how to hold
The big punch till the proper time,
Jab away with accurate rhyme;
Adapt the style or be knocked cold.
But first the groundwork must be done.
Those poets who have never learnt
The first moves of the game, they can't
Hope to win.
         Yet here comes one,
No style at all, untrained and fat,
Who still contrives to knock you flat.

19

Mike Barlow

Rolling

His canoe's state-of-the art, custom fitted:
grablines, throwlines, velcro loops, you name it.
White water's his element, drawn to stoppers and boils
like a caddis fly. A capsize brings a screw roll
so accomplished you'd think it was staged.

Only when he's beached, prising his body
from the cockpit do you notice
the shrivelled leg, the wetsuit loose and baggy,
then the shuffle, the half hop to keep his balance
and the rolling limp exaggerating sea-legs.

We stop for a pint, take a stroll by the river.
The muddy path eels its way as we follow
a dipper's bob and flit upstream. At the weir
we look into a silver crease, the broad mane of foam.
Get that wrong he says *you'll not know which way's up.*

Suddenly he's down, foot caught in a tree root.
A parachutist's roll this time and a full glass of ale slipped
from one hand to the other with the timing of an acrobat.
Before I know it he's bounced upright again,
crooked legs and crooked smile, not a drop wasted.

John Arlott

Cricket at Worcester, 1938

Dozing in deck-chair's gentle curve,
Through half-closed eyes I watched the cricket,
Knowing the sporting press would say
"Perks bowled well on a perfect wicket".

Fierce mid-day sun upon the ground;
Through heat-haze came the hollow sound
Of wary bat on ball, to pound
The devil from it, quell its bound.

Sunburned fieldsmen, flannelled cream,
Looked, though urgent, scarce alive,
Swooped, like swallows of a dream,
On skimming fly, the hard-hit drive.

Beyond the score-box, through the trees
Gleamed Severn, blue and wide,
Where oarsmen "feathered" with polished ease
And passed in gentle glide.

The back-cloth, setting off the setting,
Peter's cathedral soared,
Rich of shade and fine of fretting
Like cut and painted board.

To the cathedral, close for shelter,
Huddled houses, bent and slim,
Some tall, some short, all helter-skelter,
Like a sky-line drawn for Grimm.

This the fanciful engraver might
In his creative dream have seen,
Here, framed by summer's glaring light,
Grey stone, majestic over green.

Closer, the bowler's arm swept down,
The ball swung, pitched and darted,
Stump and bail flashed and flew;
The batsman pensively departed.

Like rattle of dry seeds in pods
The warm crowd faintly clapped;
The boys who came to watch their gods,
The tired old men who napped.

The members sat in their strong deck-chairs
And sometimes glanced at the play,
They smoked and talked of stocks and shares,
And the bar stayed open all day.

John Arlott

To John Berry Hobbs on his Seventieth Birthday
16 December 1952

There falls across this one December day
The light remembered from those suns of June
That you reflected in the summer play
Of perfect strokes across the afternoon.

No yeoman ever walked his household land
More sure of step or more secure of lease
Than you, accustomed and unhurried, trod
Your great, yet little, manor of the crease.

The game the Wealden rustics handed down
Through growing skill became, in you, a part
Of sense, and ripened to a style that showed
Their country sport matured to balanced art.

There was a wisdom so informed your bat
To understanding of the bowler's trade
That each resource of strength or skill he used
Seemed but the context of the stroke you played.

The Master: records prove the title good:
Yet figures fail you, for they cannot say
How many men whose names you never knew
Are proud to tell their sons they saw you play.

They share the sunlight of your summer day
Of thirty years; and they, with you, recall
How, through those well-wrought centuries, your hand
Reshaped the history of bat and ball.

23

James Berry

Fast Bowler

Batman's nervous wait — not a bowler's worry.
Upright wickets taunt him.
Back turned. He walks on.
A journey, long, long and steep.
Eleven men toss one ball with his arm.
Yet, ball speaks *his* eloquence.
He turns. He trots. He runs. Big long limbs
fly with pounding hoofs to a leap,
releasing a bullet of a ball.
Batsman ducks. Shelters in lower air.
Okay. Okay. Next time.

Back turned. Slowly, he walks, journeying.
Each wicket stands there — an enemy soldier.
That bat on guard. A fortress door.
Ball in hand is his charge
to despatch a man.
Ball stamps the pages of a life.
He turns. He trots. He runs. Big long limbs
fly with pounding hoofs to a leap,
releasing a bullet of a ball.
Batsman pad up. Two columns of pads.
Okay. Okay. Next time!

Back turned. Slowly, he walks, journeying.
Ball in hand is a nation's voice.
Jibes of standing wickets bite him.
Ball — *be* hurricane-powered!
He turns. He trots. He runs. Big long limbs
fly with pounding hoofs to a leap,
releasing a bullet of a ball.
Batsman hits him. Hit his ball away for four.
Loose ball. Avoid that. Avoid that.

Back turned. Slowly, he walks, journeying.
Ball tests hard how two nations can rub.
Sometimes with a spear disguised, sometimes
with a sword, gaming in an open field is
a battle, but *open*. And eyes watch him while
so erect, lordly wickets mock him.

Improvised ball, go now, arrive unreadable.
A baffler with the tricks of a genius.
He turns. He trots. He runs. Big long limbs
fly with pounding hoofs to a leap,
releasing a bullet of a ball.
Batsman hits him. Hits his ball away for six.
Unbelievable. Unbelievable. Think. Think!

Back turned. Slowly, he walks, journeying.
Wickets together. An immovable barrier.
Ball unravels an opening by combat.
Ball demands a total testing.
Eyes of his team rest on him heavily.
He turns. He trots. He runs. Big long limbs
fly with pounding hoofs to a leap,
releasing a bullet of a ball.
He misses the wickets by a pinpoint.
His missile! *His* missile! Controlled!
Launch it. Launch it, again, Launch it!

Back turned. Slowly, he walks, journeying.
Fine clothes get full of a downpour:
his fit limbs are heavy with fatigue.
But his arm works his nation's arm!
So knock him for ones and knock him for twos.
Have him glided to the boundary
or fly gone past the keeper. Have him
give a wide, a no-ball, a catch dropped,
and a spell without a wicket, and remember,
always, his next ball will carry his plan.

He turns. He trots. He runs. Big long limbs
fly with pounding hoofs to a leap,
releasing a bullet of a ball,
shattering the wickets to scattered sticks.
Got him! Got him! Let him walk.
O let him walk away, dead!

Jean 'Binta' Breeze

on cricket, sex and housework

I have never liked ironing

but there's something steamy here
that softens the crease
and although I played it straight
I fell
to your googly

I came out slightly crinkly

perhaps it's the strange things
your fingers do
around my seams

Jean 'Binta' Breeze

Song for Lara

is a young generation
comin dung sweet
nat in awe of *Wisden*
nat studyin defeat

a fresh clean page
from an islan of dreams
a bat in han an
burstin at de seams

de wicket holds no shadows
of what cannot be reached
Jus
practisin, dread,
gettin better all de time
de limelight doan mean nutten
wid a bat in mi han
liftin up mi head
an thinkin bout de glory
is a sure way to be out
before de en a de story

if de bowler fine a reason
ah will answer wid a rhyme
any kine a riddim
in mi own time

        Pan man, hole tight.
Lara een
im tekkin up im guard
fus one straight back
dung de pitch
Dis is between we an de Lord!

We bus out a heaven gate today
wid a certain majesty
buil a hero to open space
from all dat crampin' we

lightnin flash troo de covers
breakin de boundary
den we sekkle back pon de riddim wid a
Nooooo... defensively

Dance it, Lara, dance it
de march deh pon we foot
steady timin
watchful eye
wait for de tenor pan
to fly
lash it
cause it overpitch
bruk a man han
if im try ketch it
is a four, is a six, is a sure ticket
anyting ah have, Lawd,
ah gamble it

dem slow gung de riddim now, mi son,
so steady timin, bassman, come!
deh sayin we don't like it slow
deh call we calypso cricketers
say we cyaan hole dung tempo
so we sen for David Rudder now
is a ballad in kaiso
so slow...so slow
a ballad in kaiso

"Come mek we rally...y...y...y
rally rung de West Indies"

29

an wen we wear dem dung again
we gawn forward extempo

is a pair a eye dat see de ball
before de howler   tink it

a pair a leg dat dance wid ease
anywhere he   lan it

a pair a han dat have more joint
dan jus elbow   an wris

is a fella dat will fine de gap
instead a mindin it
instead a mindin it

an all de time
he smilin sweet
gentle, humble
dress well neat
bat like a ratchet
in he han
slicin troo
de hard red heat

     an he playin hiself
      he playin hiself
but he doan play all hiself yet

     he playin hiself
      he playin hiself
but he doan play all hiself

yet

Adrian Buckner

Cricket at Thrumpton

Lined up behind boundary flags
a fleet of Renault, Nissan and Ford;
only one or two from the village now
close enough to pedal or walk.

One of the old hands regrets the lack
nowadays of spectating wives and kids —
"Folk just don't have the time — always
something else they'll need or find to do."

The midday heat unfurls across a balmy
late afternoon — what fades for an hour or two
is the significance of change — absorbed
like tomorrow's heat into a reddening sky.

Long past the casting of the die, the game
ambles on without a trace of impatience;
courtesies are exchanged between men of sixteen
and sixty, a little light applause

for a manful effort at an impossible catch.
Something, eroding perhaps, is being passed on
as an unseen cow lumbers over to chew
the wing mirror of the fast bowler's Mondeo.

Wendy Cope

The Cricketing Versions
(for Simon Rae)

"There isn't much cricket in the Cromwell play."
(Overheard at a dinner-party)

There isn't much cricket in *Hamlet* either,
There isn't much cricket in *Lear*.
I don't think there's any in *Paradise Lost** —
I haven't a copy right here.

But I like to imagine the cricketing versions
Laertes goes out to bat
And instead of claiming a palpable hit,
The prince gives a cry of "Howzat!"

While elsewhere the nastier daughters of Lear
(Both women cricketers) scheme
To keep their talented younger sister
Out of the England team,

And up in the happy realms of light
When Satan is out (great catch)
His team and the winners sit down together
For sandwiches after the match.

---

*Apparently there is; *"Chaos umpire sits,/
And by decision more embroils the fray."*
Paradise Lost, Book II, Lines 907-908

Although there are some English writers
Who feature the red leather ball,
You could make a long list of the plays and the books
In which there's no cricket at all.

To be perfectly honest, I like them that way —
The absence of cricket is fine.
But if you prefer work that includes it, please note
That now there's some cricket in mine.

S.J. Litherland

Bad Light

The ruffled flags, deep bank of trees under gloom,

cold eddies of air, the swaddled wicket,
no-one sitting on the terraces,

this the coal face of a dank dark day,
the Riverside windy bowl unstirred

by strokes, empty of attention. Members sit
at white clothed tables hoping. Nasser's opening.

Held onto like a talisman.

This the place of slow appreciation
and the contemplation of the circle.

Only those who keep the game are here,
no TV, no crowds, no glamour,

the enactment of a rite passed on
by rules, history and pleasure.

The verse patterns that weave
the great battles and small,

the slow heroic sweep of epic time,
each delivery a line in stanzaic overs,

runners crossing like harpists' hands,
each delivery point and counter point,

34

question and reply like an ancient choir.

Batsmen flamboyant as chiefs
who fought battles in couplets of poetry.

The strung out fielders set as a trap,
as one by one the bowlers

connive to lure these heroes
to the pavilion. It's what keeps us waiting,

patience learnt like the ancient art of listening.

Bad light stops play: Durham v. Essex

John Lucas

An Irregular Ode on the Retirement of Derek Randall, Cricketer
for Ben

My Batter at the Bridge, tun-voice-and-booted Randall,
who in presumptuous youth once chose to long-man-handle
Shuttleworth, Lever and Simmons – Lancs' gruff and
    grudging trio –
and won for Notts a match they'd hoped to draw, *con brio*.
At the non-striker's end Great Garfield Sobers stood
to grin applause at cover drives that in due season would
drive Lillee so distracted he'd steeple at your head,
though "no use aiming there, mate, there's nowt in it,"
    you said,

"try pitching 'em up." He did. And your Centenary
innings flowed, a two days' binge, golden, crisp and buttery.
Yet oh, what homecoming waited on that wondrous 174:
Your Trent Bridge Test, and run out by the uncallipygian
    bore
Boycott. But then a county game at his own Headingley,
he prods to cover, sets off, and the "coiled cobra" he
had not considered zaps him with wit, speed, grace,
those Son-of-a-Gunn gifts you poured into summer's space.

All shirt tail, pads skew-whiff, slewed cap and Grock's
    slumped walk,
"The Sun Has Got His Hat On" you'd mourn or scatter talk
wide as fielders, bat parsing each ball in optative
mode: "I choose to cut or pull, to sweep or glance or drive,"
while stripe-tied types snuffed gin, muttering "Crackers
in one's opinion. Chap's not one of Us." True! And Packer's
Circus couldn't corral you, nor did you make bold
with Greig, Gooch and Gatting to stuff your boots
    with randgold,

but once again Down Under upped to bemused Brearley:
"Only ten minutes more, skip, it'll be fifteen to tea";
and care thus summoned, dispensed with care three
    plush fours
to hoist your hundred, sink Hogg, and become fit cause
of Arlott's measured words: "He made the method men
    look sad."
And so you did, and such sweet madness had spectators glad
hand you to pavilions, who knew the back-page scandal:
you were too rare a player for England, dear Derek Randall.

Norman Nicholson

The Field

Let me first describe the field:
Its size, a double acre; walled
Along the north by a schoolyard,
West by a hedge and orchards; tarred
Wood railings on the east to fence
The grass from the station shunting lines,
That crook like a defensive ditch
Below the ramparts of the Church;
And south, the butter meadows, yellow
As fat and bumpy as a pillow,
Rumbling down the mile or more
That slopes to the wide Cumbrian shore,
With not a brick to lift a ban
Between the eye and the Isle of Man.
A common sort of field you'll say:
You'd find a dozen any day
In any northern town, a sour
Flat landscape shaped with weed and wire,
And nettle clump and ragwort thicket —
But this field is put by for cricket.
Here among the grass and plantains
Molehills matter more than mountains,
And generations watch the score
Closer than toss of peace and war.
Here, in matches won and lost,
The town hoards an heroic past,
And legendary bowlers tie
The child's dream in the father's lie.

This is no Wisden pitch; no place
For classic cuts and Newbolt's verse,
But the luck of the league, stiff and stark
With animosity of dark
In-grown village and mining town
When evening smoke-light drizzles down,
And the fist is tight in the trouser pocket,
And the heart turns black for the want of a wicket.

Or knock-out cricket, brisk as a bird,
Twenty overs and league men barred —
Heels in the popping crease, crouch and clout,
And the crowd half-codding the batsmen out.
Over the thorn and elder hedge
The sunlight floods, but leaves a ledge
Of shadow where the old men sit,
Dozing their pipes out. Frays of light
Seam a blue serge suit; gnats swarm,
And swallows dip round the bowler's arm.
Here in a small-town game is seen
The long-linked dance of the village green:
Wishing well and maypole ring,
Mumming and ritual of spring.

David Phillips

Pyjama Pickle

For playing in the one day game
I have to wear pyjamas with my name
emblazoned on the back so punters
know their Olive Oyls from Billy Bunters.

And stunning is my suit of green,
in play-school it would make the scene,
but I play for a pickle co.
whose range of products everyone must know:
horseradish, scotch egg, gherkin, saveloy —
I bat and bowl in their employ.

I think the hype and razzmatazz
demeans the game and all their gear has
made me look not up-to-date and cool
but reinforced the archetypal flanelled fool.
Call me stuck-up and call me fickle
but I hate playing as a pickle.

Neil Rollinson

Deep-Third-Man

The infield is for wisecrackers, pepper-pots, gum-poppers:
the outfield is for loners, onlookers, brooders...
Stuart Dybek, "Death of the Right Fielder"

I like it here, where the meadows of Kent
lap at the boundary rope, redundant
with apples and hops. You can ponder
the subtler things: the way a summer
ripens with every innings, sycamores moving
through deeper and deeper greens.
A man could drop dead out here
in the long grass, and no-one would know.
They never found Blenkinsop, fielding
at deep-square-leg. They found some bones
the following year, his name carved in a tree,
but nothing more. We're a different breed.
Not for us, the tense excitement
of silly-point or forward-short-leg,
the flamboyance of bowlers
with their googlies and flippers.
I do bowl sometimes, for an over or two,
a languid, deceptive leg break;
but I pine for the stillness,
the silence of lost cricket balls
rotting like toadstools under a fence.
Nothing else happens, for months.
A whole season can pass
like a lifetime. I lounge in the sun,
practise my golf, or read a book.
You lose touch out here.
I watch the weather: the clouds,
the twelve degrees of turquoise

41

you find in an August sky,
and I love the rain, the way it soaks the hills,
the orchards, the whole of England.
One of these days they'll find me
dead among the dandelions,
the red smudge of a cricket ball
gracing my head, or maybe I'll disappear
into the unmown grass, the oaks
and elm trees, the last day of summer,
into memory, and beyond.

Alan Ross

Cricket at Brighton

At night the Front like coloured barley-sugar; but now
Soft blue, all soda, the air goes flat over flower-beds,
Blue railings and beaches; below, half-painted boats, bow
Up, settle in sand, names like Moss-Rose and Dolphin
Drying in a breeze that flicks at the ribs of the ride.
The chalk coastline folds up its wings of Beachy Head
And Worthing, fluttering white over water like brides.
Regency Squares, the Pavilion, oysters and mussels and gin.

Piers like wading confectionery, esplanades of striped tulip.
Cricket began here yesterday, the air heavy, suitable
For medium-paced bowlers; but deck-chairs mostly were vacant,
Faces white over startling green. Later, trains will decant
People with baskets, litter and opinions, the seaside's staple
Ingredients. Today Langridge pushes the ball for unfussed
Singles; ladies clap from check rugs, talk to retired colonels;
On tomato-red verandas the scoring rate is discussed.

Sussex v. Lancashire, the air birded and fresh after rain,
Dew on syringa and cherry. Seaward the water
Is satin, pale emerald, fretted with lace at the edges,
The whole sky rinsed easy like nerves after pain.
May here is childhood, lost somewhere between and never
Recovered, but again moved nearer like a lever
Turned on the pier flickers the Past into pictures.
A time of immediacy, optimism, without stricture.

43

Post-cards and bathing machines and old prints.
Something comes back, the inkling and momentary hint
Of what we had wanted to be, though differently now
For the conditions are different, and what we had wanted
We wanted as we were then, without conscience, unhaunted,
And given the chance must refuse to want it again.
Only, occasionally, we escape, we return where we were:
Watching cricket at Brighton, Cornford bowling through
    sea-scented air.

Siegfried Sassoon

The Blues at Lord's

Near-neighboured by a blandly boisterous Dean
Who "hasn't missed the match since '92",
Proposing to perpetuate the scene
I concentrate my eyesight on the cricket.
The game proceeds, as it is bound to do
Till tea-time or the fall of the next wicket.

Agreeable sunshine fosters greensward greener
Than College lawns in June. Tradition-true,
The stalwart teams, capped with contrasted blue,
Exert their skill; adorning the arena
With modest, manly, muscular demeanour —
Reviving memories in ex-athletes who
Are superannuated from agility —
And (while the five-ounce fetish they pursue)
Admired by gloved and virginal gentility.

My intellectual feet approach this function
With tolerance and Public-School compunction;
Aware that, whichsoever side bats best,
Their partisans are equally well-dressed.
For, though the Government has gone vermilion
And, as a whole, is weak in Greek and Latin,
The fogies harboured by the august Pavilion
Sit strangely similar to those who sat in
The edifice when first the Dean went pious —
For possible preferment sacrificed
His hedonistic and patrician bias,
And offered his complacency to Christ.

Meanwhile some Cantab slogs a fast half-volley
Against the ropes. "Good shot, sir! O good shot!"
Ejaculates the Dean in accents jolly.....
Will Oxford win? Perhaps. Perhaps they'll not.
Can Cambridge lose? Who knows? One fact seems sure;
That, while the Church approves, Lord's will endure.

Chris Searle

Balthazar's Poem

I was born a white boy
   in a white boy's world.
I never met a black man
    except Man Friday
    and whispers of the Mau-Mau.
When I was ten in the London suburbs
they covered me with black boot polish
all over arms, face, legs
    put a crown on my head
and I was the King of Ethiopia,
Balthazar they called me
    bringing myrrh to Jesus —
whatever that was, they never told me.
It took a month to rub the blackness off
and I was chapped and red and raw like pigmeat.

The first black man I ever met
was a man called Wesley Hall.
I was thirteen
    he was an unknown sportsman
on his first tour of my country.
I asked for his autograph at Ilford Cricket Ground
as he stood, shy and huge
    smiled, and wrote for me.
I loved him.

47

Then his friend Gilchrist came whirling
pounding, stamping, hurling
he bowled bullets at my countrymen.
This was sport, but something else too.
He moved with a fury
        an anger like a storm
like the Mau-Mau he was a soldier
like the men in Malaya he was a guerrilla
like the warriors in Cyprus he was a hero
a new world was rising in the tornado of his arms
the trajectory of his hurling was at the heart of all things evil.

Then a man named Collie Smith
        swung his bat like a sword
he had a sword in his hand
and something new was sweeping England's turf
something heavier was rolling the ground

and cutting from the past.
When Wes bowled
        magnificence was born for me
I never knew it before
I tried, I strove, I imitated
I found my own way,
        my own action
and every time I hurled
        I sought to touch his power.

Now I have lived in black lands of freedom
made common ground by systems of love,
the mist of history is clearing
and Balthazar's polish seems to take a new hue
and ground from the skin
        deep into my flesh and bone
the truth is forever growing —
Gilchrist's Caribbean is our common ground
The mountains of Ethiopia are our common ground
Ilford Cricket Ground is our common ground
The earth of tomorrow is our common ground.

Gopi Warrier

Cricket at Lords

Living behind Lords
I don't have to be
at the grounds or watch TV
to know the score.

Each time there is grand
applause England has scored a four.
Polite applause is the opposition's
six. A deafening roar that shakes
the house is an Aussie wicket
or the LBW of Tendulkar.
Pin-drop silence means England
wickets are falling like ninepins.

Last summer, by the lake in Regents Park
birds singing, world bright
and cheery I pass
a short, balding man in a fading three piece,
barrister's brief case underarm.
Perhaps an old Harrovian cricket fan.
He walks slowly, "a schoolboy with his satchel"
and a heavy heart.

On his boyish face is gloom.
The bright day
cannot touch his heart normally languid in the sun.
Obviously England has lost the Match.
Sadly I let him pass knowing his grief
but still long to commiserate
him for a sunny day
when all was perfect
except the score.

49

P.G. Wodehouse

Missed!

The sun in the heavens was beaming;
The breeze bore an odour of hay,
My flannels were spotless and gleaming,
My heart was unclouded and gay;
The ladies, all gaily apparelled,
Sat round looking on at the match,
In the tree-tops the dicky-birds carolled,
All was peace till I bungled that catch.

My attention the magic of summer
Had lured from the game — which was wrong;
The bee (that inveterate hummer)
Was droning its favourite song,
I was tenderly dreaming of Clara
(On her not a girl is a patch);
When, ah horror! there soared through the air a
Decidedly possible catch.

I heard in a stupor the bowler
Emit a self-satisfied "Ah!"
The small boys who sat on the roller
Set up an expectant "Hurrah!"
The batsman with grief from the wicket
Himself had begun to detach —
And I uttered a groan and turned sick — It
Was over. I'd buttered the catch.

Oh ne'er, if I live to a million,
Shall I feel such a terrible pang.
From the seats in the far-off pavilion
A loud yell of ecstasy rang.
By the handful my hair (which is auburn)
I tore with a wrench from my thatch,
And my heart was seared deep with a raw burn
At the thought that I'd foozled that catch.

Ah, the bowler's low querulous mutter,
Point's loud, unforgettable scoff!
Oh, give me my driver and putter!
Henceforward my game shall be golf.
If I'm asked to play cricket hereafter,
I am wholly determined to scratch.
Life's void of all pleasure and laughter;
I bungled the easiest catch.

Kit Wright

Cricket Widow

Out of the love you bear me,
  By all its sweet beginnings,
Darling heart, please spare me
  The details of your innings.

Kit Wright

*I Found South African Breweries Most Hospitable**

Meat smell of blood in locked rooms I cannot smell it,
Screams of the brave in torture loges I never heard nor
    heard of
Apartheid I wouldn't know how to spell it,
None of these things am I paid to believe a word of
For I am a stranger to cant and contumely.
I am a professional cricketer.
My only consideration is my family.

I get my head down nothing to me or mine
Blood is geysering now from ear, from mouth, from eye,
How they take a fresh guard after breaking the spine,
I must play wherever I like or die
So spare me your news your views spare me your homily.
I am a professional cricketer.
My only consideration is my family.

Electrodes wired to their brains they should have had
    helmets,
Balls wired up they should have been wearing a box,
The danger was the game would turn into a stalemate,
Skin of their feet burnt off I like thick woollen socks
With buckskin boots that accommodate them roomily
For I am a professional cricketer.
My only consideration is my family.

---

*Graham Gooch

They keep falling out of the window they must be clumsy
And unprofessional not that anyone told me,
Spare me your wittering spare me your whimsy,
Sixty thousand pounds is what they sold me
And I have no brain. I am an anomaly.
I am a professional cricketer.
My only consideration is my family.

Jeremy Duffield

Cross-country Runners

Someone snitched!
Some teacher's pet, some cross-country freak:

In the changing-room it was
Jim, me, and the rest limbering up,
pushing out of the door,
fanning into the yard, pacing ourselves,
finding places as we jogged down the drive.
By the school gate
Jim and I were trailing,
watching the rest turn right, set off down the road,
while we turned left,
ran ten yards and opened the red telephone-box door.

In the distance the rest filed over a stile,
set off up the hill, into the trees,
while we hunkered down, lit up, inhaled deeply
and waited.

Thirty minutes of stories, jokes, pressing button B
then we walked across the road,
swished knee-high through scrub and ragwort
to the far hedge.
Leaders appeared, then groups, then stragglers.
We joined mid-pack, panting with the rest,
arrived back close to the lead, headed for the showers.

Until,
shivering one winter's day in the steamed-up booth,
cupping our hands round cigarette tips,
the door opened,
"Out!"

Wyatt, in tracksuit and flexing a slipper,
"Out! And up that bloody hill!"
The slipper stung,
and through the crisp drifts ice raked thighs,
numbed toes, fingers,
chilled the heart.

Last home, wet through
we showered to jeers, flicked towels.
Cross country runners!

Stanley Cook

Racing Cyclist

His feet clipped to it, he turns the treadmill
Of his double chain wheel, in highest gear.
The early morning mist on the level road
Through a low-lying countryside
Retreats before him, dragging its cloak
Over the hedges, the lines of poplar trees
And towns and villages with cheering crowds,
The sun, like everyone else, coming out to watch.
For miles, he himself and the riders beside him
Seem to him to be standing still,
All moving at the same high speed.

Under welcoming banners and past advertisements,
Low on the handlebars, he ducks the air
That blocks his way and clutches at his clothes,
Keeping level above all with himself
And not a second behind the best he can do.

He rides as surely as if his narrow tyres
Fitted into a groove already there
Or followed a chalk line drawn to the finish
Where people leap up at the roadside,
Beckoning and calling a winner out of the pack.

Louise MacNeice

The Cyclist

Freewheeling down the escarpment past the unpassing
   horse
Blazoned in chalk the wind he causes in passing
Cools the sweat of his neck, making him one with the sky,
In the heat of the handlebars he grasps the summer
Being a boy and to-day a parenthesis
Between the horizon's brackets; the main sentence

Waits to be picked up later but these five minutes
Are all today and summer. The dragonfly
Rises without take-off, horizontal,
Underlining itself in a sliver of peacock light.

And glaring, glaring white
The horse on the down moves within his brackets,
The grass boils with grasshoppers, a pebble
Scutters from under the wheel and all this country
Is spattered white with boys riding their heat-wave,
Feet on a narrow plank and hair thrown back

And a surf of dust beneath them. Summer, summer —
They chase it with butterfly nets or strike it into the deep
In a little red ball or gulp it lathered with cream
Or drink it through closed eyelids; until the bell
Left-right-left gives his forgotten sentence
And reaching the valley the boy must pedal again
Left-right-left but meanwhile
For ten seconds more can move as the horse in the chalk
Moves unbeginningly calmly
Calmly regardless of tenses and final clauses
Calmly unendingly moves.

Neil Rollinson

The Semis

After a skinful of beer you become one
with the darts, bright as a monk fishing at dawn,
the treble 20 large as a lake.
Zen and the art of 50l. You stand at the line
and watch the arrows spin through the smoke:
sixty, a hundred and twenty, one hundred and eighty!
The last match of the South London pubs'
semi-final and you're playing a stormer.
The corned beef sandwiches taste like salmon,
the beer like Veuve Clicquot, and even the barmaid
is stunning tonight. You preen your feathers, polish
the tungsten tips of your darts, and step to the mark.
You focus your mind: there is only the board,
the bull's-eye, blood-red and open, everything else
fades to a blur. A hundred and forty-two required.
You do your sums: treble 18, double 19, a bull to finish.
You see them off; the dart's instinct for flight
you imagine: neither a throw, nor a letting go.
They bed themselves in where you want them,
fifty-four, ninety-two, you watch the last dart home,
like a smart-dart, to the dead centre. Double bubble!
You're into the finals. You finish your beer
in a single gulp, and now you are through
your mind lets go. Your eyes glaze over.
You're seeing two doors to the gents, two platefuls
of sausage rolls, and two barmaids beaming at you
as you slide to the floor. You lie on your back
watching the ceiling-rose spin through the smoke,
a prayer wheel, a mandala cured in nicotine.

Peter Sansom

If You Can't Finish, You're Buried

You asked about the darts.
The big one, starting
Huddersfield fortnight.

Once the whole town emptied,
met on the prom at Scarborough and Cleethorpes.
They put on special trains.

Now they do gardens, or decorate,
grip hand-luggage
as the plane gains altitude
and the man in the hat points out
it is a beautiful day after all

above the clouds.
Perhaps it is always sunny in Spain.

But in Marsden I hit tops —
miscounting, wanting 32,
and he chips out on 106.
Second leg I go off on tons and a one-forty,
missing bull for a twelve-darter.
For no reason I am shaking

and have nine darts at a double
before he puts it away. He smiles,
throwing first in the next,

"You'll not come back from here, kid."
And I don't. The plane dips:
it's pouring after all
in Alicante; the nettles have seeded
the neighbour's lawn,
and there's still the back-bedroom to do.

I am thirty and I have a beard:
I hate it when they call me kid.

Elaine Feinstein

Fishing

In leaf dust, and tarred wood
the chestnut, radiant as a moving tiger
the willow falling like water spilt
yellow-green in the river: my son
sits rocking eagerly, his
arms holding his knees as I
watch the bob of his float, the changes

of moving water, moving lips and his
bright eye. He is watching for
a single gudgeon to fly up
out of the silver mud, but when
he turns, smiling

in the delicate line of his
neck I sense uncertainly how
fierce a passion he
is holding back in
his still silence.

Seamus Heaney

The Salmon Fisher to the Salmon

The ridged lip set upstream, you flail
Inland again, your exile in the sea
Unconditionally cancelled by the pull
   Of your home water's gravity.

And I stand in the centre, casting.
The river cramming under me reflects
Slung gaff and net and a white wrist flicking
   Flies well-dressed with tint and fleck.

Walton thought garden worms, perfumed
By oil crushed from dark ivy berries
The lure that took you best, but here you come
   To grief through hunger in your eyes.

Ripples arrowing beyond me,
The current strumming water up my leg,
Involved in water's choreography
   I go, like you, by gleam and drag

And will strike when you strike, to kill.
We're both annihilated on the fly.
You can't resist a gullet full of steel.
   I will turn home fish-smelling, scaly.

Ted Hughes

Eighty, and Still Fishing for Salmon

He holds
The loom of many rivers.
An old rowan now, arthritic, mossed,
Indifferent to man, roots for grave.

He's watching the Blackwater
Through hotel glass. Estuary nets
Empty. The river fishless. He's a trophy
Of the Great Days — his wrinkles, his tweeds,

And that armchair. And the Tussaud stillness.
Probably he's being tossed
Across a loch on Harris.
Both worlds have been lost

By the ritual mask
That hangs on its nail.
Soon he'll be out there, walking the sliding scree
Of the river — and over and over

His fly will come round on the vacant swirl.

An old Noh dancer, alone in the wind with his dance.
An air-fed, mountain prayer-wheel
Loyal to inbuilt bearings, touch of weather,
Though the heavens fail.

64

Michael Laskey

Sea-Anglers

Always there before us, green umbrellas
draw us to the anglers standing, arms crossed,
mindful of horizons and their rod-tips
but, beyond a nod, indifferent to our curious
clumping over pebbles through their silence.

Lost on them, our glance of admiration
at tackle-boxes trim in all compartments,
our eye caught by their bait: lug, undulant
and gleaming; on newspaper a mackerel
unfreezing, one flank sawn off down the backbone

with an old steel knife. Still life. We move on
down the beach. What are they hoping to catch?
Cod's what they'd say if pushed. And whiting, flats.
I can see one there quietly unscrewing
a thermos, imagine one lighting his lamp.

Andrew Motion

A Severe Absence of Fish

Even the most masterful of Zen Grand Masters
might lose patience and want time to run faster

if, waist-deep like me in this bitterly cold river
all week, he had cast his truest cast over and over —

casting with all the passionate concentration of will
a person can possibly have when they are trying to kill

something they love, and leaving no secret lie
untouched by the slick, expressionless, heartless fly,

no lee of a dark rock, no pool, no plausible run,
no mysterious shadow, no patch of sleepy sun —

which means (remember: I'm casting over and over)
all day my head is my own, intent on the river,

and also clean off my shoulders, full of whatever else
might come along next: the wall-eyed head of a grilse

an otter chewed off and left on its feasting stone
bleakly to catch the light; then the otter alone

and playing, in and out of the water so fast, so deft
am always agog at the place it has suddenly left;

then one silly Canada Goose flying miles above my head,
the creak of its wing-beat like you turning over in bed.

Yes, that's right. What comes along next. One thing
just slithering after another like beads down a string

and away into nothing, the nothing that day after day
I carefully enter and wade through, finding a way

to bring its cold surface to life, to fill empty space
with a rising, drawn, dead-pan, strenuous face reflecting
    my face.

E.J. Scovell

The Boy Fishing

I am cold and alone,
On my tree-root sitting as still as stone.
The fish come to my net.   I scorned the sun,
The voices on the road, and they have gone.
My eyes are buried in the cold pond, under
The cold, spread leaves; my thoughts are silver-wet.
I have ten stickleback, a half-day's plunder,
Safe in my jar.   I shall have ten more yet.

Subhadassi

Fishing

I tackle-up. My mind's all carp: slick slow-movers
mottled with leather, or mirror. We're armed to the teeth
with par-boiled potatoes and honey, a killer
combination, but this morning nothing's biting.

An aeon later, frozen, walking legs like someone else's
up the steps, I look back to find the pond haloed
by spindles of silver birch; catch one big spare rib of a ripple
sounding its length. I'm spell-bound. Something's stirring.

Daniel Weissbort

*A Jew Watches You Fish**

I leaned against a rock
as you fished.
It was quite straightforward,
the line cast,
the fly drawn back across the current.

This seemed perfunctory to me.
Or had it been simplified, for my benefit?
I didn't think so, such was not your way —
just that the ritual was well-established.

Once, twice you nabbed a salmon,
said I brought you luck.
I told myself I was a kind of mascot —
a Jew and the fish with blood on its lips!

At this moment of strictly limited horizons,
of silenced protest,
I scurried as it were, between ghettos.

The way was windy, the flesh crawled in vain,
as I watched you cancel the living thing
with a blow to the brain.

---

*From a sequence of poems, Letters to Ted

70

Allan Ahlberg

Friendly Matches

In friendly matches
Players exchange pleasantries
Hallo, George!
How's the Missus?
Admire opponents' kit
Smart shirt, Bert!
Sympathise with linesmen
Difficult decision, there.
And share their half-time oranges.

In friendly matches
Players apologise for heavy tackles
How clumsy of me.
And offer assistance with throw-ins
Allow us to help you with that heavy ball.

In friendly matches
Players and substitutes alike
Speak well of referees
First-rate official
Sound knowledge of the game
Excellent eyesight!

In friendly matches
Players celebrate opposing players' birthdays
With corner-flag candles
On pitch-shaped cakes.

In friendly matches
Players take it in turns
No, no, please, after *you*

to score.

Kevin Cadwallender

A Game of Two Halves

A division three morning
in a division four town
a thousand footballs ago.

He was the first
black man I'd ever seen
and the terraces
didn't care only booed
when he missed a sitter
or got too greedy.

After blowing his chance
in first division reserves,
after screwing some Director's wife,
he got relegated to this turf.

Later on
in the 'pictures'
we'd see him sleeping
off the drink,
Sleeping off
the missed opportunities,
Slipping a cross
into a non-league goal.

Brendan Cleary

Brian's Fables

How come I'm starting to feel more distant, like a pop star,
when I meet up with the old Eagles team in The Whitecliff?

They can remember all my antics on the pitch better
than I can. "Arthur, you're a fuckin onion" I shouted

because he was useless & that time I took my shirt off
& handed it to the psycho full-back saying "here, have it",

when he fouled me & the day there was a minute's silence
for some league official so the Ref blew his whistle

& the Prof went steamin down the wing shouting for the ball,
he had to walk back feeling a right eejit & we cracked up

& there was that game on a cow field at the back of Carnlough,
Fat screaming at the specky Ref who didn't book him, no way,

didn't send him off either, just ripped out the corner flag,
ran at him & threatened to "carry his fuckin head off!"

& I had to be called Brian when we played away fixtures,
at least in some places, say in Ballyclare where the Dirts

in their bomber jackets waved Red Hands & Union Jacks
behind the goalposts weren't anything abnormal & fights

were many & games got abandoned & once the old Whitehead team
had to leap in their cars, escape with their kit still on.

Brian has stuck with me since. I've always needed an alias
& all this floods back to me as I dander about, & steamin

someone like D.J. rolls over, grips my arm & asks me:
"Boutya Brian, how long are ye home for."

& I think "more like how long before I get away!..."

73

Mandy Coe

Live Match — Big Screen

One hand against the tiles,
the other spidering into his flies,
a man sways cursing: lost chances,
the slippery slide down leagues and tables.
Stepping out, still zipping, he blinks in the smoke,
then staggers back to his seat.

Up among remnants of dusty tinsel,
projector beams ghost and curl
as back and forth the action slides
across the big white screen.

And in a blaze of noise, the pitch is here,
halogen-lit: each blade of grass,
each clod of dirt; the steaming breath
of players rising with the stadium roar.

Every eye is fixed, narrowed to this;
a pub full, they light up, sway, heads
shove, willing the right spin, the right...
"Go on you bastard!"
  "Go ON!"
    They lean in,
      half rise;
        beer spills,
          the ball...
            the ball...
misses. Punctured
they fall back as one,
tugging at pinching trousers
and slapping banter back and forth.

A woman wipes the bar at the back,
wipes round elbows, under glasses.
Not having to smile, she is thinking.
Alone for a moment, behind their backs.

Andy Croft

Methuselah's Losers

A quick one-two, a turn, a screaming shot,
  Back off the post, a run through the defence
To knock it straight back in, and though we've not
  Yet touched the ball, we're one-nil down against
A team whose youth and energy subdues us
And makes us feel a hunch of hopeless losers.

Because Methuselah's too long to go
  On Third Division league and fixture lists
We play as Losers and/or Meths — as though
  We only lose because we're always pissed!
There's better teams than us made up of boozers,
And being sober's no help to the Losers.

At least we are consistent; losing streaks
  Like ours take years and years of bloody training,
It's hard to be this bad, you need technique;
  So please don't get me wrong, we're not complaining,
We don't think being useless helps excuse us,
It's just that practice makes us perfect losers!

You do not have to win to feel the buzz
  Of sweat, testosterone and self-display;
Part circus show (including clowns like us),
  Part theatre, part athletics, part ballet,
A game designed for gents that's played by bruisers
Who are long past their prime (just like Meths Losers).

I like defeat, its sweaty, human smell,
    Familiar as a much replayed own goal
Or spannered shot; this losing fits me well
    (Just like our too-tight strip!) and on the whole
I think a winning sequence would confuse us,
At least you know just where you are with losers.

While those who can afford it cheer success
    Via satellite TV and sponsors' boxes,
On sweaty 5-a-side courts we transgress
    The age's most unbending orthodoxies:
To be the worst! The thought somehow renews us:
Down with success! And up with all the losers!

Not coming first's an honourable aim
    When winning is the only Good; there's pride
In coming last, in losing every game,
    In being always on the losing side.
The games we really should have won accuse us:
Success belongs to others, not to losers.

Let's hear it then for those who're past their best;
    Without us there would not be many winners,
We're here to make the numbers up, the Rest,
    To teach the art of losing to beginners;
Their shiny, bright successes just amuse us,
For even winners have to play with losers.

So here's to hopeless losers everywhere
    Who know we're stuffed before we even start,
Who live with disappointment and despair,
    Who turn defeat into a kind of art;
An army of dissenters and refusers,
We'd change the world — if we weren't such good losers!

Simon Curtis

Gloucestershire Alliance, 1985

Reading the sports page through, I see
That Tewkesbury Rovers went two up
Last week, at Wick, through goals by Lea;
That Wilmcote won the John Wood Cup;

But Adlestrop — *they* crashed 4–1
At home to Chadlington, it seems,
Positioned here (some *cachet* gone)
Among the local soccer teams

Of Oxfordshire and Gloucestershire.
So Evening *Stars* and *Mercuries*
Encompass matches everywhere
In small print mid-March summaries —

A bit like hawthorn hedged about
Rough pitches marked on rec and field
Year after year close-mapping out
Dense worlds of Trophy, Cup and Shield.

Near clinker lanes, allotment ends,
By pond and pylon, swing and slide,
Flower marginal and countless grounds
For fellowship, all England-wide,

Evoking countless memories
Now, as in twenty-, fifty-five,
Of shot, save, tackle, move and miss:
Quixotic, teeming, rich, alive.

Turf hushed tonight, in dark and dews,
Under perennial, damp-charged sky;
Where ghostly figures, stamping shoes,
Watch ghost-teams fight their needle tie.

Alan Dent

This Sporting Life

Because I had a good right foot
And could run a bit
They put me on the wing.
And I was happy out there
Away from the general ruck.
If the ball came to me, I'd scoot
Could beat a wooden full-back,
And even scored the occasional goal.
But I was always happier somehow
Playing three-and-in with
A couple of mates,
Or even a solitary game of walley
Savouring that curious ping of
A frido against brick.
No team-spirit, they said,
And dropped me from the side.
So I took my ball
Ran to the park
Kicked it high
Watched it float and drift
And where it fell
Trapped it
Neatly
And purely
For my own delight.

Rosie Garner

On Football and Killing Chickens
21st June 2002

So I'm standing at the bus stop, stunned and only half
    awake.
All I know is, it's 2:1 to Brazil and not over yet.
It'd been 1:1 at the cob shop, shutters up but no
    customers,
we might as well be muffled by a foot of snow.
At the post office they watched it on the black and white,
nervous as another break in.

It was Owen who'd woken me up — the roar from the
    factory
I'd thought it was on fire again — then I'd remembered.

So now I'm on the bus next to a woman
telling me about killing chickens in Jamaica,
performing post mortems on hens.
She said her husband used to work at Boots,
heavy manual — had to be dragged off every shift.
Big man, strong man. And then he got thin,
and she knew before he did, before the doctors did —
because of things the chickens taught her.

She said they got so thin the wind blew them over.
She found kinks like bent fingers in the intestines,
coconut straw in the gizzards.
Fascinated her to the knife point.

So she knew before anyone.
If he'd lived they might have —
she gets off at the Chinese wholesalers.

And then we're in town and I know it's over.
Don't have to ask. Can't ask.
Streets full of people and I'm walking
into a wall of sadness,
The end of the World Cup.
A man leans against the railings on Parliament Street
opposite a flag in a café window. He can't look at it —
has to stand opposite it.
He's too weak to stand.
Somebody comes over to him, could be anybody,
stands really close, doesn't put his arm round
but the arm's there. Tender.

And I'm standing here alone, with this misery
lapping over my ankles, it's sucking me in,
I'm loosing my grip and I have to remember,
this, has nothing to do with me.
If there was a wind, it would blow me over.

Martin Green

Ode to Hackney Marshes

Twenty-two sins, said Auden, here have lease;
In our case the sin is to play badly
What the East-enders do with greater ease.

For ninety Sunday-morning minutes, sadly
Or sometimes gay, we chase the ball across
A Lowry landscape, where we swear madly

At the deaf referee, whose whistle's boss,
Trying to keep our sins within the lease
Of the white lines which make a slip a loss.

There are moments of joy; the Golden Fleece
Is putting the ball past the netless post;
A rare occurrence and a short-lived peace.

Energy we have, what we lack the most,
Skills that surge in our minds but do not show;
Our brilliant shots most often hit the post.

However the running and the swearing go
The walk back to the dressing room is like
Napoleon's retreat from burnt Moscow.

The bitterness as we approach the dike
Hangs on us like a straggling moustache
(Perhaps it's suffering we really like?).

Next Sunday we will come to Hackney Marsh
To cast our hopes upon the field of play;
The wages of twenty-two sins is harsh.

Mike Harding

Daddy Edgar's Pools

Each muggy Saturday you sat still while the set
Called out into the hushed room where I sat
With burning ears and heard a London voice
Call names as strange as shipping forecasts through the air:
Hamilton Academicals, Queen of the South,
Pontefract United, Hearts of Midlothian,
Wolverhampton Wanderers, Arbroath, Hibernian,
And once, I thought, a boy called *Patrick Thistle.*

Then every week after the final check,
When Friday's dreams were scratched out with a squeaky pen,
You took down from upstairs your brass band coat,
Gave me the wad of polish and the button stick.
And there in that still, darkened room I polished up
Each brassy button world that showed my face;
While you on shining tenor horn played out
Your Thursday Millionaire's lament
For a poor man's Saturday gone.

Each week you, Thursday Millionaire, would conjure up
The juju, stab the coupon with a pin
Or read the cups, perm my age and height
With Hitler's birthday and the number of
The bus that passed the window and the clump
Of pigeons on the next door neighbour's loft.
With rabbit's foot, white heather, and wishbone
You fluenced the coupon that I ran to post.

83

Tony Harrison

Divisions

All aggro in tight clothes and skinhead crops,
they think that like themselves I'm on the dole.
Once in the baths that mask of 'manhood' drops.
Their decorated skins lay bare a soul.

Teenage dole-wallah piss-up, then tattoos.
Brown Ale and boys' bravado numbs their fright —
MOTHER in ivy, blood reds and true blues
against that North East skin so sunless white.

When next he sees United lose a match,
his bovvers on, his scarf tied round his wrist,
his rash NEWCASTLE RULES will start to scratch,
he'll aerosol the walls, then go get pissed...

So I hope the TRUE LOVE on your arms stays true,
the MOTHER on your chest stays loved, not hated.

But most I hope for jobs for all of you —

next year your tattooed team gets relegated!

Ian Horn

In the Moonlight a Football

The moon is an *Azzurri* blue;
the colour of Italy.
On the night of the full-lunar eclipse
Frank pronounces *La Luna*
in broad Glaswegian.

At Frank's Fish & Chip Shop
small talk is dominated by
Inter Milan, Glasgow Celtic,
or the woeful Scottish goalkeeping
on TV the other night.

In the back-room is an archive
of books, photographs, programmes,
and Ronaldo's left-boot.
Salt & Vinegar seeps through
the news print of Match Reports.

Between frying times we discuss
the clan system of warrior culture on the terraces
and West Highland league tables.

My appetite for a fish supper
is on hold, substituted
for the Football World of Frank Arrighi.
The mobile rings Verdi,
"30 million Lira for a donkey!"
Frank's blood
is Frying Tonight.

Michael Horovitz

from *The Game* section of *The Wolverhampton Wanderer*

......to the epicure stillness, stadium hush
  that succeeds the dying-down drone of corpse crush
...Mush of ticket touts, cub reporters, wolf-scouts
Barkers, unofficial programme louts —
Ice-cream men, hot dogs, oompah bandolineers
Motley tipsters, majorettes, gawky-gracious peers

— Solempne procession of crimsonbraid strumpeters
— Battallions of Thousands Abide with Thee
— Thousands on thousands insatiate embattled
On all sides, bright-scarved, riddling berattled
Air thick inlaid with pomp of parade
— Cameradoes connected in voice invoke
Insistent, exhorting — ill augurs, go broke!
— Strike up, kick off, wax fertile Glad Band
— Hoarse blurts, nameless contact in Oneness, ground
United through instincts closer than fog
(That caps the scene to
                dim dome of a gasworks
  — as seen from the wide berth of distant skyplanes.
  Radio plugs in and the telly explains
But it's *in*side you feel the irresistible tide
Breaking wave over wave)
                as side by side
Onward the regnant rockers ride,
Sweep the field and subside a whole township's plush pride
Like some pregnant phalanx-unbridled steed bride
— Delivered, relaxed — gunpowder contracting —

Apocalypse blurt
                 of prescient tense heap'd-up anticipation
— One foot put wrong may mean relegation
   — OUR MAN'S HURT – bites the dirt – dread desolate cries
— Reserves cringe and tremble
                     — to quit conturbation

Step in dauntless
         — & | Equalise |

Let the news spread wiresped jubilant host

   Stop-press amplified coast to coast —
We're ahead, We're the Most — Allelluia Halloo
   In unison Yoicks Huzza-yawp WE'RE THE WOLVES —

   — Steeples of choirs people Goodyear tyres,
Chubb's safety-locks & the Willenhall stocks
As Walsall-ball tunes vamp Wulfrunian runes

   ...Wondering ear-views, Wolverine beer blues
Wulvering Heights, Villa-woof delights
Turn again to regain — London's Orient well met
— Nor let me forget, at Hampton yet:

Many the Hamptons drawn to play
— Hampton Wick — perfum'd garden,
   Northampton Southampton Hampton-in-Arden

Lionel Hampton — Hampton Court — great Littlehampton
Big Teaming Hampton Agonistes — Wolves
                              — Ye Pimpernel Pack Ye Glee
  — Swiftshuffling past bottomrung'd Hammers v. Pompey,
Trampoleaning the ladder the decks and the docks
Husky-galloping flashmolten socks
                  — Atalan-
                          ticking over
                          ball-crazed
                                  hoof-humdingers
      — Jets of Mullen-skrim, Jumping Jim — Finney
          Phantastickle wingers —
          Jaggery shaggery Symphony Sid
— Sped by Billy Wright
                              — the Gridiron Sidespin Kid —
Billy
  — knight errant of "might for right" —
Wirehaired campaign-brain Vikingshock Header—
    Albion's All-time good bloke Leader
          *Un*perfidious   — terrier
                          stormtrooping bleeder...
Later, cuplinked laurel-baided goal-chain'd O'points meant
    He won —
              the hot seat at Highbury
— Order of Boot   worth well mikel a ton!
    Cherouted auld wolfery,
Toasting his pals with that skill-bruited loot
— Open-hampering hampers of bootfruit lopp'd full
From stalwart plum orchards ripe seasons topped

...Greyhound-spawned Wembly-lawn'd mummer's
    memory sufficed
(Tho juiced in his gorrillorialisted cups) to store
A new pack with devises of wolflore galore
                          begaurrrh

— Stern conclaves — Venerable veteran coach
   In holly and ivy league with trainers
   ...After workouts the lads lay massaged, footsore —
Warmed by his pep stalks of sage, hard-won wage
   & steaming world onion-bowl galumphing glaze

         as qwhan, a mere Whelp, a pup —
      Tup-kinzossled how He, Ironwrought skip
         Angelically bootskulled that entire '51 Eleven-ship
         to League-*And*-Cup's top-tip — All Heaven's trip —

...But for the Arsenal's tried, & justly famed
   Reserve of hothouse power:
No wenlock of wasps zap-suction'd that flower
   — Turreted amphitheatric brawn-mower

In fumy face of which Whirr-wolves abandoned grope
...Tho every match struck spurr'd afresh
                              the Challenge —
To light up — flash out momently each half the finest hour
— What use, against our red **and** white-hot shower! —
Come throstle drops or shine, aye — whate'er the sky
   — Outshimmering turnstile-riot storm's eye
   Whether ball-love hove leather enginedrawn
By mute and glory-be namelost pawn
— Or juttingjawed thrusty ruggerbugger Punchkonck
Rolls Razorsharp-shooter — Ronnie Rooke! — Or swart
      "Bighead" Compton — Indestructible custodian
      Of the Penalty Area Fortress — whose bell-clear kick
Would fairground-hammer clang his brother Denis off
Ball
      battening a crazy cricket-neck
                              line
                                 to the cornerflag

Thereat to pull his left leg back,

                                 & Slice the leather orb

— Whizzing up   and — split-

                            -secondly stock still

At the dead shed centre of the goalmouth

                                 (just south of

                                 the totterers

— For Doug Lishman's bonce to bounce it deftly d

                                      o

                                    w

Athwart their 'keeper's   n

                    despairing

                              muzzlehanded

                                      dive —

...Dream-machine of a team —

Each man a Genius, each content — for

"Modest in Victory, Cheerful in Defeat" —

   to be obscene — to be Seen I mean

   — a small but gaily gleaming cog

       Even where, in wet or midwinter season

       The bed lay rampled to a murky bog

   — Or frrosted over — hard as glacier-ramparts —

They'd brace themselves,

   Wolf Mannioned as the Nordic Middlesburghers,

   In most likewise hard and strongboned harmony —

Erect through storm,

                    and failure of omened truth-to-form

— Like as if they were

Not London's gunmen grappling wild-wolves

   — Not eleven men at all

       But co-ordinated limbs of One Man

       Labouring as 'twere

               in every prime of Wife.

90

Ted Hughes

Football at Slack

Between plunging valleys, on a bareback of hill
Men in bunting colours
Bounced, and their blown ball bounced.

The blown ball jumped, and the merry-coloured men
Spouted like water to head it.
The ball blew away downwind —

The rubbery men bounced after it.
The ball jumped up and out and hung on the wind
Over a gulf of treetops.
Then they all shouted together, and the ball blew back.

Winds from fiery holes in heaven
Piled the hills darkening around them
To awe them. The glare light
Mixed its mad oils and threw glooms.
Then the rain lowered a steel press.

Hair plastered, they all just trod water
To puddle glitter. And their shouts bobbed up
Coming fine and thin, washed and happy

While the humped world sank foundering
And the valleys blued unthinkable
Under depth of Atlantic depression —

But the wingers leapt, they bicycled in air
And the goalie flew horizontal

And once again a golden holocaust
Lifted the cloud's edge, to watch them.

91

Mike Jenkins

The Pwll Massacre

We're playing high above the tundra zone
v. Pwll Boys' Club under 14's
on a pitch shared by sheep,
horse-riders, motorbike scramblers
and more dogs than Crufts.

We're in with a chance
till we count our team:
nine players including three keepers,
two of our star defenders
have discovered lager at 13
and there's no way to wake them.

Pwll are a small team
with the best (and only) oranges half-time.
They even have a tea-urn,
which is useful in the Arctic circle
somewhere north of Asda's.

We play a mystery formation
including at least seven strikers.
The pre-match team-talk involves
"It's a game of two halves,
but not equal players!"

It's their ref and he's fair
as the weather. At 4-0 down
we're heading for their goal
only to be whistled for off-side...
our manager's warned for swearing,
their parents give him verbals
like snowballs packed with stones,
a collie brings light relief
with the most adept footwork
since Stanley Matthews...

At 12-0 down I give up counting:
the game's lost its point
because the local paper
only report the first ten!
We score a consolation
when the collie deftly noses in.
It's disallowed as he's underage
and anyway, hasn't signed the forms.

The ref plays twenty minutes extra time
so his son can get a hat-trick.
Pwll parents are all gloating
like polar bears watching
a load of rabbits fishing.
"Ne' mind, son," I say after,
"at sea level you'd have won!"

Tom Leonard

Yon Night

yonwuz sum night
thi Leeds gemmit Hamdin
a hunnirn thurty four thousan
aw singing
yilnivir wok alone

wee burdnma wurk then
nutsnur a wuz
but she wuzny intristid
yi no thi wey

well there wuzza stonnin
ana wuz thaht happy
ana wuz thaht fed up
hoffa mi wuz greetnaboot Celtic
anhoffa mi wuz greetnaboot hur

big wain thata wuz
a kin laffitit noo

John Lucas

What Holds Them

"Move over God — Cloughie's coming"
(Message written on a card and left among the thousands of
tributes that arrived at the City Ground after news reached
Nottingham of the death of Brian Clough.)

Brian Clough is gone, red-carded by cancer.
Rough-tongued shaman, rogue, blest necromancer
who blazed new life into clubs, players, teams —
losers no more but playing out their dreams
as tricksters. "Get rid of racists!"
Brian's order. "We've done with fascists.
And by the way, no swearing gentlemen."
And the Trent End sang "the referee's an orphan."

He coaxed their wit, gave thumbs up to a pride
they hugged like trophies captured by each side
he set free for the joy of it. "The best
manager England never had," some claim,
which may be so, although a fairer test
of worth than braggadocio sports-page fame
is that, of thousands packing the Market Square
to mourn this day, half have no love of the game
he loved, but all loved *him*, that cross-grained, rare
man whose sending off's brought them to fill
this place for one last time and holds them still.

Sunday, 3 October, 2004

Ian McMillan

Home Support

It is mid-July, 1997. It is hot.
Barnsley are in the Premier League,
and in my head our season
is laid out as simple as an Underground Map,
or a child's drawing of the solar system.
Mid-July, a pre-season friendly
against Doncaster. The start of something
and one of my daughters is coming to Doncaster
on her own for the first time on the bus
to meet me to go to the match. As the bus
rolls into the bus station I see her red shirt
upstairs, and she waves, and my heart breaks

for her, and me, and her red shirt with 21 TINKLER
on the back, and the bus driver who is a Middlesbrough fan,
and the other people who tumble off the bus in their red shirts
with the season laid out in their heads simple and lovely
as a map of the solar system or a child's drawing
of the Underground, and the Greek bus station toilet attendant
who knows me and shouts PREMIER LEAGUE, but
mostly it breaks for her, and me, and her red shirt.

Still, it's July. It's hot. We meet Chris and Duncan
and we try to go into a pub even though my daughter's
a bit young and a man in a suit says Sorry, Home Support Only.
And my heart breaks

for her, and me, and her red shirt, and the Home Support
who cheer Doncaster and whose season is laid out simple
as a serving suggestion, or a child's drawing of a football team,
but mostly it breaks for her and me.

We get a taxi home, which seems extravagant, but I think
of the Greek toilet attendant and I shout PREMIER LEAGUE
on our path as we walk into the house, father and daughter, red
shirt, hot night, Home Support, season laid out in our heads
simple and lovely as a football programme, simple and lovely
as a penalty kick, a well-taken corner.

Adrian Mitchell

By the Waters of Liverpool

So many of her sons drowned in the slime of trenches
So many of her daughters torn apart by poverty
So many of her children died in the darkness
So many of her prisoners slowly crushed in slave-ships
Century after red century the Mersey flowed on by —
By the waters of Liverpool we sat down and wept.

> But slaves and the poor know better than anyone
> How to have a real good time
> If you're strong enough to speak
> You're strong enough to sing
> If you can stand up on your feet
> You can stomp out a beat...

So we'd been planning how to celebrate
That great red river of Liverpool
As our team rose to a torrent
That would flood the green of Wembley
We'd been planning how to celebrate
The great red dream of Liverpool
For Dalglish held the Cup in his left fist
And the League in his right —
By the waters of Liverpool we sat down and wept.

Our scarves are weeping on the gates of Anfield
And that great singing ground is a palace of whispers
For the joy of the game, the heart of the game,
Yes the great red heart of the great red game
Is broken and all the red flowers of Liverpool —
By the waters of Liverpool we sat down and wept.

April 1989, after Hillsborough

98

Sean O'Brien

Cantona
from *Sports Pages*

One touch, then turn, then open the defence,
Then, gliding down your private corridor,
Arriving as the backs go screaming out,
You slide into slow motion as you score
Again, in the heroic present tense.
As Trevor says, that's what it's all about.

Like boxing and the blues, it's poor man's art.
It's where the millions possess a gift
As vital as it looks vicarious:
While Fergie chews and struts like Bonaparte
We see the pride of London getting stiffed,
And victory falls on the Republic, *us*.

But Eric, what about that Monsieur Hyde,
Your second half, who grows *Les Fleurs du Mal*
Who shows his studs, his fangs and his disdain,
Who gets sent off, then nearly sent inside
For thumping jobsworths at the *Mondiale*?
Leave thuggery to thugs and use your brain:

Now choose the spot before the ball arrives,
Now chest it, tee it, volley from the D.
Now Wimbledon, like extras, simply look,
And even Hansen feels he must agree:
This "luxury" is why the game survives,
This poetry that steps outside the book.

Sean O'Brien

Football! Football! Football!
from *Sports Pages*

My sporting life (may I refer to me?)
Was never all it was supposed to be.
Mine was a case of talent unfulfilled.
I blame society, which blames my build.

From trap and pass and backheel in the yard
To deskbound middle age is something hard
For the Eusebio of '64
To grasp: you don't play football any more.

Your boots and kit are all gone into dust,
And your electric pace a shade of rust.
Whatever knocks the football fates inflict
On Shearer now, your chance of being picked

If England reach the Mondiale in France
(Does Umbro really make that size of pants?)
Is smaller than the risk of being brained
By frozen urine falling from a plane,

And though you'll stop by any rainy park
To watch folks kick a ball until it's dark,
You don't expect Dalglish will seek you out
To ask you what the game is all about.

But more fool him, you secretly suspect:
You've seen the lot, from Crewe to Anderlecht,
From Gornik to Stranraer to River Plate,
The Cosmos and Montrose and Grampus Eight,

The Accies, Bochum, Galatasaray,
Finbogdottir, Dukla Prague (away),
Botafogo, Bury, Reggiana...
Football! Football! Football! Work? *Mañana.*

Sponsored by IKEA and by Andrex,
Butch in sacks or mincing on in Spandex,
The great, the mediocre, the pathetic,
Real Madrid and Raggy-Arse Athletic —

Twelve quid a week or fifty grand an hour,
The game retains the undiminished power
To stop the clock, accelerate the blood
And sort the decent geezer from the crud.

From 5-3-2 to Kaiser Franz libero
Is there a team formation you don't know?
Experience! There is no substitute
When working out why Andy Cole can't shoot.

The fields of dream and nightmare where the great
Line up beside the donkeys to debate
Who gets the league, the cup, the bird, the chop
And whether Coventry deserve the drop

Are graveyards of a century's desire
To keep the youth that sets the world on fire —
Pele's '58, Diego's '86,
And Puskas hushing Wembley with his tricks...

And back, and back, to James and Meredith
And all the tricky Welsh who took the pith,
Until West Auckland marmalize Juventus —
World on world through which the game has sent us,

Until at last we stand in some back lane.
You're Cantona but I'll be Best again.
Who gives a toss what any of it means
While there are Platinis and Dixie Deans?

There life is always Saturday, from three
Till *Sports Report*, as it's supposed to be,
The terrace in its shroud of freezing breath,
Hot leg, crap ref, a soft goal at the death,

Fags and Bovril, bus home, bacon sandwich —
Paradise in anybody's language
Is listening for the fate of Stenhousmuir
(Robbed by Brechin 27-4).

Mark Robinson

Rio de Juninho

We could have had a gritty midfield battler,
cast from the bits British Steel had left over,
last welding done by a returner from Saudi,
dragged from Grangetown by a traveller's pony,
his forehead trailing on the dirty tarmac,
a matter of inches from his hairy knuckles,
his mam and dad proud and loud in the stand
when his prehensile studs rip carefully through
the arty-farty shins of a Dutch dazzler,

or a rough and tumble striker on the way up,
thick as a brick made of slag but big hearted,
with a forehead like a stoker's shovel
and sharpened elbows that have been known
to carve his names in defender's backsides,
whose first words as a child were translated as
"I'll bite your bloody balls off you big arsewipe",
with a right foot as true as his tax returns,

but then we would not have seen,
walking by the still filthy river one day,
ten thousand yellow shirts dancing in the breeze,
a new look in people's eyes,
something not to be denied even by results,
that I know is ridiculous and still want,
a dreaming set off like a ticking bomb,
this chipped and battered town
twinned with a place so exotic
we did not know it was just like home.

Neil Rollinson

The Penalty

The stadium comes to a hush;
it is so quiet you can hear a light-bulb
hum to itself in the dressing room.
You carry the ball in your hands,
your palms are sweating, you feel nauseous.
The goal-mouth rushes away.
You can just see, in the distance,
the white glow of the cross-bar,
the German keeper waving his arms.
You can hear him shouting:
Schaffst du nicht, du Wichser.
You settle the ball on its spot.
Do you place it, or blast it?
If you miss this kick you're finished,
your team-mates will sink to their knees
in the grass. You step back from the ball.
Schaffst du nicht, the keeper repeats.
You take a run. You are running all day
and night. When you get to the ball
you are weak with the effort.
You swing your leg, your foot
finds what you think is a perfect purchase,
the crowd goes wild, they rise in a wave
behind the goal. You watch the ball —
you can't believe where it goes.

Michael Rosen

Unfair

When we went over the park
Sunday mornings
To play football
we picked up sides.

Lizzie was our striker
because she had the best shot.

When the teachers
chose the school team
Marshy was our striker.

Lizzie wasn't allowed to play,
they said.

So she watched us lose, instead...

105

George Szirtes

Preston North End

Tottenham Hotspur versus Preston North End.
Finney's last season: my first. And my dad
with me. How surprisingly well we blend

with these others. Then the English had
the advantage, but today we feel
their fury, sadness and pity. There were some bad

years in between, a lot of down-at-heel
meandering. For me though, the deep blue
of Preston was ravishment of a more genteel,

poetic kind. They were thrashed 5-1, it's true,
and Finney was crocked by Mackay. Preston went down,
hardly to rise again. But something got through

about Finney the plumber, Lancashire, the Crown,
and those new days a-coming. The crowd dissolves,
but we are of the crowd, heading into town

under sodium street lights. This year Wolves
will win the title. Then Burnley. I will see
Charlton, Law and George Best. The world revolves

around them and those voices on TV
reading the results. I'm being bedded in —
to what kind of soil remains a mystery,

but I sense it in my marrow like a thin
drift of salt blown off the strand. I am
an Englishman, wanting England to win.

I pass the Tebbitt test. I am Allan Lamb,
Greg Rusedski, Viv Anderson, the boy
from the corner shop, Solskjaer and Jaap Stam.

I feel no sense of distance when the tannoy
plays Jerusalem, Rule Britannia or the National Anthem.
I know King Priam. I have lived in Troy.

Keith Wilson

Another Littlewoods Carling Coca Cola Milk Cup Uncle Joe's Mint Balls Semi-Final Second Replay Tetchy Terse Ticket Knock-Back

Having queued on a full bladder
without complaint, butties, bickies or a tartan flask
for at least five and a half hours plus stoppage time
I finally make it to your little portakabin window

I snuggle up to the plug-hole in the perspex
uncurl a well-rehearsed, if slightly inane, introductory smile
speak slowly and clearly through the little perforations
and without looking up, you tell me I'm not on

> I chew a semi-splutter and I swallow a cough
> and weigh up the possibilities of maybe kicking off
> but I resist the urge to nut the glass and with much
> emphasis on diction
> I calmly fondle my worry beads and say with some
> conviction

I've got the four special vouchers
three yards of industrial strength gusset elastic
sixteen Curley Wurley wrappers from the seventies
five ticket stubs against teams into marmite and Crazy Frog
ringtones
two jars of "No Frills" extra large pickled gherkins
four chunky hand-knitted toilet roll covers
and a fully working mechanised otter

There's a sharp intake of breath involved as you shake
your head
like a plumber sizing up a tricky no-job-too-small
while preparing the way for the two-footed
two-fingered-jaw-dropping estimate

108

How can I be discarded
dismissed, red-carded
ineligible and persona non grata?
I go every single game
through the wind and through the rain
I should be lauded and applauded as a martyr

You look up from your indifference
sigh one of those sighs that plague the terminally
   inconvenienced
lean forward and, through what looks like a wind-induced
   half-smile, say —

This is charades and fan cards
and postal applications
adult and child re-unions
"Category A" inflations
executive leg room up-grades
for the battery hen stand
and the official supporter's club credit card
with the highest APR in the land
this is for those paying through the nose
for a seat with an obstructed view
so you're wasting your time here, fella
you're in the wrong bleedin' queue

I'm rooted to the spot — drained, tired and dull
overcome with a confusion that adds a calmness to the lull
and as I try to disguise an Elvis leg 'cos I'm bursting for a pee
you lob your voice over my head in the general direction of not
   me

"NEXT!" you shout
convincingly

Gwyneth Lewis

A Golf-Course Resurrection

Mid morning, above the main road's roar
the fairway's splendid — eighteen holes
high on a mountain, which should be all slope,
too steep for a stretch of evenness or poise.
By logic this layout shouldn't work at all
but all the best places are untenable
and the greens are kind as mercy, the course
an airy, open paradox.

The golfers move like penitents,
shouldering bags and counting strokes
towards the justices of handicap and par.
The wind, as sharp as blessing, brings its own tears.
Just out of sight is the mess below:
deconsecrated chapels, the gutted phurnacite,
tips reshaped by crustacean JCBs,
tracts of black bracken that sent the night on fire.

There is a light of last things here.
These men have been translated from the grime
of working the furnace with its sulphur and fire
into primary colours and leisurewear.

They talk of angles, swings and spins.
Their eyes sprout crows' feet as they squint to see
parabolas and arcs, an abstract vision, difficult to learn,
harder to master, but the chosen ones
know what it is to play without the ball
when — white on white — against the Beacons' snow
the point goes missing, yet they carry on
with a sharper focus on their toughest hole,
steer clear of the bunkers, of their own despair,
sinking impossible shots with the softest of putts
still accurate, scoring an albatross
as around them the lark and the kestrel ride
on extravagant fountains of visible air.

U.A. Fanthorpe

Hang-gliders in January
(for C. K.)

Like all miracles, it has a rational
Explanation; and like all miracles, insists
On being miraculous. We toiled
In the old car up from the lacklustre valley,
Taking the dogs because somebody had to,
At the heel of a winter Sunday afternoon

Into a sky of shapes flying:
Pot-bellied, shipless sails, dragonflies towering
Still with motion, daytime enormous bats,
Titanic tropical fish, and men,
When we looked, men strapped to wings,
Men wearing wings, men flying

Over a landscape too emphatic
To be understood: humdrum fields
With hedges and grass, the mythical river,
Beyond it the forest, the foreign high country.
The exact sun, navigating downwards
To end the revels, and you, and me,
The dogs, even, enjoying a scamper,
Avoiding scuffles.

It was all quite simple, really. We saw
The aground flyers, their casques and belts
And defenceless legs; we saw the earthed wings
Being folded like towels; we saw
The sheepskin-coated wives and mothers
Loyally watching; we saw a known,
Explored landscape by sunset-light,

We saw for ourselves how it was done,
From take-off to landing. But nothing cancelled
The cipher of the soaring, crucified men,
Which we couldn't unravel; which gave us
Also, somehow, the freedom of air. Not
In vast caravels, triumphs of engineering,
But as men always wanted, simply,
Like a bird at home in the sky.

John Betjeman

Hunter Trials

It's awf'lly bad luck on Diana,
  Her ponies have swallowed their bits;
She fished down their throats with a spanner
  And frightened them all into fits.

So now she's attempting to borrow.
  Do lend her some bits, Mummy, *do*;
I'll lend her my own for to-morrow,
  But to-day *I*'ll be wanting them too.

Just look at Prunella on Guzzle,
  The wizardest pony on earth;
Why doesn't she slacken his muzzle
  And tighten the breech in his girth?

I say, Mummy, there's Mrs. Geyser
  And doesn't she look pretty sick?
I bet it's because Mona Lisa
  Was hit on the hock with a brick.

Miss Blewitt says Monica threw it,
  But Monica says it was Joan,
And Joan's very thick with Miss Blewitt,
  So Monica's sulking alone.

And Margaret failed in her paces,
  Her withers got tied in a noose,
So her coronets caught in the traces
  And now all her fetlocks are loose.

Oh, it's me now. I'm terribly nervous.
  I wonder if Smudges will shy.
She's practically certain to swerve as
  Her Pelham is over one eye.

* * *

Oh wasn't it naughty of Smudges?
  Oh, Mummy, I'm sick with disgust.
She threw me in front of the Judges,
  And my silly old collarbone's bust.

John Betjeman

Upper Lambourne

Up the ash-tree climbs the ivy,
  Up the ivy climbs the sun,
With a twenty-thousand pattering
  Has a valley breeze begun,
Feathery ash, neglected elder,
  Shift the shade and make it run —

Shift the shade toward the nettles,
  And the nettles set it free
To streak the stained Carrara headstone
  Where, in nineteen-twenty-three,
He who trained a hundred winners
  Paid the Final Entrance Fee.

Leathery limbs of Upper Lambourne,
  Leathery skin from sun and wind,
Leathery breeches, spreading stables,
  Shining saddles left behind —
To the down the string of horses
  Moving out of sight and mind.

Feathery ash in leathery Lambourne
  Waves above the sarsen stone,
And Edwardian plantations
  So coniferously moan
As to make the swelling downland,
  Far-surrounding, seem their own.

Philip Larkin

At Grass

The eye can hardly pick them out
From the cold shade they shelter in,
Till wind distresses tail and mane;
Then one crops grass, and moves about
— The other seeming to look on —
And stands anonymous again.

Yet fifteen years ago, perhaps
Two dozen distances sufficed
To fable them: faint afternoons
Of Cups and Stakes and Handicaps,
Whereby their names were artificed
To inlay faded, classic Junes —

Silks at the start: against the sky
Numbers and parasols: outside,
Squadrons of empty cars, and heat,
And littered grass: then the long cry
Hanging unhushed till it subside
To stop-press columns on the street.

Do memories plague their ears like flies?
They shake their heads. Dusk brims the shadows.
Summer by summer all stole away,
The starting-gates, the crowds and cries —
All but the unmolesting meadows.
Almanacked, their names live; they

Have slipped their names, and stand at ease,
Or gallop for what must be joy,
And not a fieldglass sees them home,
Or curious stop-watch prophesies:
Only the groom, and the groom's boy,
With bridles in the evening come.

117

Kevin Fegan

from *Racer*

Truth is, I've never won a TT.
I bull myself up as a champion
but I've never made it to the top
perch on the podium.
I'm 39 years old, don't know
how much longer I can go on.
So many races have come and gone
and never the champion I dreamed of,
champion of the streets, where I started,
where I come from, that's why it matters.
This time, this time I'm in with a real chance,
I was fastest in practice
so I'm first off this morning.
Every ten seconds riders are released:
they'll all start behind me,
it's up to me to keep it that way.
This is the bit I don't like:
the waiting, the butterflies.
We've made our choice of tyres:
it's wet which favours the nutters.
I like the wet, I prefer it
to the sun in my eyes,
if I can keep my bravery
this side of madness, I can turn
the occasional slides
and waivers into victory
and stay alive to ride again.
The leader boards are ready,
the white triangular clock is ticking,
I look around at the grandstand
on one side of the road
and the cemetery on the other,
preparations are underway:

the white church is being cleaned
and fresh plots are being turned.
A gang of Born Again Middle-Aged Bikers,
Bambis, pass innocently by the gates:
they're here in their full matching leathers
to test their Sunday dry-weather-only
riding skills with their mates
on the ultimate road race circuit.
I watch the local bobbies
in their white spiked helmets
keeping a crowd of hell's angels
with video cameras at bay.
Through a gap in the stand I can see
rows and rows of merchandising
where the long hair and the short hair,
the grey hair and the no hair,
the blond hair and the brown hair,
the red hair and the dyed hair
buy their t-shirts and cups,
baseball caps and books,
videos and magazines,
souvenir programmes and ice-creams
as the industry behind the scenes
increases year by year.
Cars have suddenly disappeared
from the face of the earth,
even a Ferrari would fail to turn heads here
Two wheels fast, four wheels last.
The teams are in their pits, ready
to pitch their wits against the road conditions,
the tyres are out of their blankets
and onto the machines,
time for a little magic of my own.
Call it superstition,
I won't allow my bike to take up position
until I've done a figure of eight,
my lucky number,
no point tempting fate, is there?

Cathy Grindrod

Taking Sides

The ball, familiar, honeycombed,
held like a shield by Susan Jones.
Lines of yellow Aertex, lime green shorts,
required socks, accurately slouched.
The netball court — its tangled web
of indistinguishable rules.
Defend Attack. Mark. Mark.

Susan Jones picks teams.
The others move ahead — right, left,
left, right, cutting the calm
of afternoon, stamping daisies into grass.
The three of us are left. That look.
Those sniggers, snorts, safe grins.
We wander to our weak point, choose.

The ball is given life; a cannon shot,
careering near. I freeze.
Balloon now, sailing overhead,
beyond these upstretched arms,
these tiptoes. Aertex riding.
At last in reach, has grown
to planet size, is dropped.

Susan Jones has words to say.
Words which stop the match.
I'm facing Susan Jones. My hand cracks
like a whiplash on her cheek. Once.
The afternoon is frozen, still,
lines of yellow, green, a once
white ball. Then from the sidelines,

shifting. We play on;
things somehow changed.

Linda France

Polo at Windsor

This is the ritual. This is the game.
There are many rules. The sun will shine.
All thoroughbreds are equal, some more
equal than others. You will be well-trained,
well-groomed. You must always look your best.
Toss your head and snort a stream of gorgeous
vowels. You may not be awfully bright,
but what you've got is class, the sheen
of sterling across your silken flanks.

You will be fed and watered at someone
else's expense on the close-clipped lawn,
till you feel the adrenalin course
through your veins, like Pimms, like champagne,
the muddy sapphire of blood. Bare your teeth,
coast, thunder, twist, foul. Darling, your life's
at stake. How many minutes of glory
while the shutters whirr, the mallets click?
Main player, you won't be ridden roughshod.

And if you're lucky, if you're a winner,
the Queen of England will stroke you
with her gloved hand. You can take home
a Cartier bauble with your aching legs,
your splitting head. Don't fret if you're hot
and steamy at the end of the day;
there'll always be someone to put you back
in your box, strip you off and bed you down.
That is the ritual. That is the game.

121

David Craig

Into Rock

He stretched to fit the rock
He crouched and eeled to fit the rock
Thinned and flexed to fit the rock
Spreadeagled on its smelted plates
Feeling his fingers hone to claws

He chimneyed up the gigantic split
Sitting in air like an ejecting pilot
While the sky out there
Blazed at him and the granite ground his spine
Then surfaced from the fissure like a mole

Bearing the chimney's pressure in his hunch
Its rising in his springing tendons
Its darkness in the gleam behind his eyes

Bearing the face's crystals in his fingerprints
Its cracking torsions in his wrists
Its drop in the air beneath his insteps

It moulded him. He was its casting.
His clay was kneaded to its bas-relief.
His brain infolded, mimicking its strata.
And when he called, and the echo heard his note,
It parodied his language.

David Craig

Life-Line

*"40 metres of 11-millimetre perlon with nylon core
(kernmantel), available in red or gold, tested for six falls"*

On the dark face a red artery pulses,
Quick and hot on the inert mineral mass,
Tensing from my waist to the unknown above.
It ripples briefly. It stills.
It bides there, quintessence of direction,
Absolute only path from here to there.

It has nosed through overhangs,
Cleft tussocks, headed slantwise,
Homing on the slatey pinnacle
Where it found no harbour,
No perch for a pigeon even
On the sloping dragon-scales.

Under the overhang it defines space
As it parts from the chopped-off facets
Of the fractured strata
And hovers, free as a falcon
Whose master lets it fly
Only so far on the looping creance.

The scarlet life-line with its sparks of blue
Crackles between me and my partner,
Signalling tremors when the toes fail
To kindle friction and the fingertips
Tighten, boosting weight barely
Against gravity's fatal magnet.

123

The line writes in red,
"Here and here your life takes moments
Round a brittle fulcrum. The last fraction
Of precarious poise is the first second
Of the next rising. You cannot grasp the point
Until you act on it, make it yours."

Elizabeth Jennings

The Climbers

To the cold peak without their careful women
(Who watching children climbing into dreams
Go dispossessed at home). The mountain moves
Away at every climb and steps are hard
Frozen along the glacier. Every man
Tied to the rope constructs himself alone.

And not the summit reached nor any pole
Touched is the wished embrace, but still to move
And as the mountain climbs to see it whole
And each mind's landscape growing more complete
As sinews strain and all the muscles knot.

One at the peak is small. His disappointment
The coloured flag flown at the lonely top,
And all the valley's motive grown obscure.
He envies the large toilers halfway there
Who still possess the mountain by desire
And, not arriving, dream in no resentment.

Graham Mort

Climbing at Heptonstall Quarry

The will of the spidering men
Has split the rock:
Gritstone sweats out their palm-grease
The sun clambers over a grey arête of cloud.

Water globules seep from the cracks,
Wobble past their sweating shoulders to
Smash on jackdaw-shit debris below.

These men are climbing into the rock,
Jamming themselves into honey-coloured, warm,
Unleavened stone with groaning insteps.

Their minds have gone dark,
Narrowed by sheer upward motion.
Rock surforms elbows, knuckles, fingertips:
All around golden faces have sheared off,
Clean and empty.

The future has no finger holds
Yet the men rise upwards, upwards, upwards
Into the lip of the overhang
Into the shadows that grip their hands and pull.

Graham Mort

Climbing With a Dead Man

The day he fell his cry grabbed at sky,
His body's dark star wheeled the void:
I held him, belayed, took the strain,
Until he climbed back past me spewing blood.

At every hold his eyes dulled with hate,
At every rest he coiled the rope's long
Hiss, betrayed to rock that bears us, that
Licks us with a black, parched tongue.

This morning we woke on the totem of the crag:
It reared dumbly, fractured, bare.
Later, sun will pinion moves across its sleep,
Our fingers sweating on its dreams of air.

He makes the moves and I follow, nudged
By thermals, testing each flake.
Questions piton deep into my stone-numb,
Fissured mind: it is days since he spoke.

I climb his chimneys slippery with blood,
Lodge my feet on red stains leaked from his toes:
He takes the rope but does not see,
His eyes torn out by screaming hawks.

The night of the day he fell, I dreamed
Of rain lashing rock, blue ropes ablaze
With lightning, St. Elmo's fire
Spidering between us on the drenched face.

127

But his shoulders were heaving towards
Some hold in that hurricane of night,
Hands bearing down to raise his body to a ledge,
Balanced on a flickering crux of light.

Now a raven comes close to watch us,
Its wing-tips scattering clouds' white spores:
It rides their solidity like waves,
Its eye sees life leaking from our pores.

I have forgotten how many days we have climbed,
His empty eyes are blind to time:
I say that we are hands on a clock-face of rock,
His purple tongue lolls and I bite mine.

He takes the rope, I gasp for it,
Face grazed against the shark-skin rock,
Sun falls back behind its splintered spines:
Each night he chooses the ledge to bivouac.

No sleep: canvas flaps with moans of the dead
Who cling to this stone needle without hope.
At dawn I ask him if he has heard their cries,
He shakes his eyeless head and coils the rope.

He makes the moves and I follow,
He gives me rope, I take it, tasting fear.
The rock twins us, hold by hold:
I see myself, the void, steps reaching into endless air.

John Betjeman

Henley Regatta 1902

Underneath a light straw boater
In his pink Leander tie
Ev'ry ripple in the water caught the Captain in the eye.
O'er the plenitude of houseboats
Plop of punt-poles, creak of rowlocks,
Many a man of some distinction scanned the reach to
Temple Island

As a south wind fluttered by,
Till it shifted, westward drifting, strings of pennants
house-boat high,
Where unevenly the outline of the brick-warm town of
Henley
Dominated by her church tower and the sheds of
Brakspear's Brewery

Lay beneath a summer sky.
Plash of sculls! And pink of ices!
And the inn-yards full of ostlers, and the barrels running dry,
And the baskets of geraniums
Swinging over river-gardens
Led us to the flowering heart of England's willow-cooled
July.

James Kirkup

Rugby League Game

Sport is absurd, and sad.
Those grown men, just look,
In those dreary long blue shorts,
Those ringed stockings, Edwardian,
Balding pates, and huge
Fat knees that ought to be heroes'.

Grappling, hooking, gallantly tackling —
Is all this courage really necessary? —
Taking their good clean fun
So solemnly, they run each other down
With earnest keenness, for the honour of
Virility, the cap, the county side.

Like great boys they roll each other
In the mud of public Saturdays,
Groping their blind way back
To noble youth, away from the bank,
The wife, the pram, the spin drier,
Back to the Spartan freedom of the field.

Back, back to the days when boys
Were men, still hopeful, and untamed.
That was then: a gay
And golden age ago.
Now, in vain, domesticated,
Men try to be boys again.

Simon Curtis

Sports Field, South Manchester

Hands numb, lungs rasping — about one-tenth alive —
I whistle up. Touch-down? Knock-on? Scrum five?
Don't know. Don't care. The try line's lost in snow,
While the wind-chill factor chills like ten below.
My borrowed boots are pinching, and they hurt.
The sweat has turned to ice inside my shirt.

"Stamp your authority on the game; you're boss"
They said. But Lord, this is ridiculous;
It's *sleeting* now. Oh I'm an ace BF
For promising to come and effing ref.
What Paradise is like, though, I see clear:
It's a long hot bath, a bar and lots of beer.

J.C. Squire

from *The Rugger Match*
(Oxford and Cambridge — Queen's — December)
(To Hugh Brooks)

III

Whistle! A kick! A rush, a scramble, a scrum,
The forwards are busy already, the halves hover round,
The three-quarters stand in backwards diverging lines,
Eagerly bent, atoe, with elbows back,
And hands that would grasp at a ball, trembling to start,
While the solid backs vigilant stray about
And the crowd gives out a steady resolute roar,
Like the roar of a sea; a scrum, a whistle, a scrum;
A burst, a whistle, a scrum, a kick into touch;
All in the middle of the field. He is tossing it in,
They have got it and downed it, and whurry, oh, here they come,
Streaming like a waterfall, oh, he has knocked it on,
Right at our feet, and the scrum is formed again,
And everything seems to stop while they pack and go crooked.
The scrum-half beats them straight with a rough smack
While he holds the ball, debonair... How it all comes back,
As the steam goes up of their breath and their sweating trunks!
The head low down, the eyes that swim to the ground,
The mesh of ownerless knees, the patch of dark earth,
The ball that comes in, and wedges and jerks, and is caught,
And sticks, the dense intoxicant smell of sweat,
The grip of the moisture of jerseys, the sickening urge
That seems powerless to help; the desperate final shove
That somehow is timed with a general effort, the sweep
Onward, while enemies reel, and the whole scrum turns
And we torrent away with the ball. O, I know it all...

I know it... Where are they?... Far on the opposite line,
Aimlessly kicking while the forwards stand gaping about,
Deprived of their work. Convergence. They are coming again,
They are scrumming again below, red hair, black cap,
And a horde of dark colourless heads and straining backs;
A voice rasps up through the howl of the crowd around
(Triumphant now in possession over all the rest
Of crowds who have lost the moving treasure to us)
"Push, you devils!" They push, and push, and push;
The opponents yield, the fortress wall goes down,
The ram goes through, an irresistible rush
Crosses the last white line, and tumbles down,
And the ball is there. A try! A try! A try!
The shout from the host we are assaults the sky.
Deep silence. Line up by the goal-posts. A man lying down,
Poising the pointed ball, slanted away,
And another who stands, and hesitates, and runs
And lunges out with his foot, and the ball soars up,
While the opposite forwards rush below it in vain,
And curves to the posts, and passes them just outside.
The touch-judge's flag hangs still. It was only a try!
Three points to us. The roar is continuous now,
The game swings to and fro like a pendulum
Struck by a violent hand. But the impetus wanes,
The forwards are getting tired, and all the outsides
Run weakly, pass loosely; there are one or two penalty kicks,
And a feeble attempt from a mark. The ball goes out
Over the heads of the crowd, comes wearily back;
And, lingering about in mid-field, the tedious game
Seems for a while a thing interminable.
And nothing happens, till all of a sudden a shrill
Blast from the whistle flies out and arrests the game.
Half-time... Unlocking... The players are all erect,
Easy and friendly, standing about in groups,
Figures in sculpture, better for mud-stained clothes;
Couples from either side chatting and laughing,
And chewing lemons, and throwing the rinds away.

133

IV

The pause is over. They part from each other, sift out;
The backs trot out to their stations, the forwards spread;
The captains beckon with hands, and the ball goes off
To volleys and answering volleys of harsher cheers;
For the top of the hill is past, we course to the close.
We've a three-point lead. Can we keep it? It isn't enough.
We have always heard their three-quarters were better than
    ours,
If they once get the ball. They have got it, he runs, he passes,
The centre dodges, is tackled, passes in time
To the other centre who goes like a bird to the left
And flings it out to the wing. The goal is open;
He has only to run as he can. No, the back is across,
He has missed him; he has him; they topple, head over heels,
And the ball bumps along into touch. They are stuck on our line;
Scrum after scrum, with those dangerous threes standing
    waiting,
Threat after threat forced back; a save, a return;
And the same thing over again; till the ball goes out
Almost unnoticed, and before we can see what is done,
That centre has kicked, he has thought of the four points,
The ball soars, slackens, keeps upright with effort,
Then floats between posts and falls, ignored, to the ground,
Its grandeur gone, while the touch-judge flaps his flag,
And the multitude becomes an enormous din
Which dies as the game resumes, and then rises again,
As battle of cry of triumph and counter-cry,
Defiant, like great waves surging against each other.
They work to the other corner, they stay there long;
They push and wheel, there are runs that come to nothing,
Till the noise wanes, and a curious silence comes.
They lead by a point, their crowd is sobered now,
Anxious still lest a sudden chance should come,
Or a sudden resource of power in mysterious foes

Which may dash them again from their new precarious peak,
Whilst we in our hearts are aware of the chilling touch
Of loss, a fatal thing irrevocable,
Feel the time fly to the dreaded last wail of the whistle,
And see our team as desperate waves that dash
Against a wall of rock, to be scattered in spray.
Yet fervour comes back, for the players have no thought for
    the past
Except as a goad to new effort, not they will be chilled:
Fiercer and faster they fight, a grimness comes
Into shoving and running and tackling and handing off
We are heeling the ball now cleanly, time after time
Our half picks it up and instantly jabs it away,
And the beautiful swift diagonal quarter-line
Tips it across for the wing to go like a stag
Till he's cornered and falls and the gate swings shut again.
Thirty fighting devils, ten thousand throats,
Thundering joy at each pass and tackle and punt,
Yet the consciousness grows that the time approaches the end,
The threat of conclusion grows like a spreading tree
And casts its shadow on all the anxious people,
And is fully known when they stop as a man's knocked out
And limps from the field with his arms round two comrades'
    necks.
The gradual time seems to have suddenly leapt...
And all this while the unheeded winter sky
Has faded, and the air gone bluer and mistier.
The players, when they drift away to a corner
Distant from us, seem to have left our world.
We see the struggling forms, tangling and tumbling,
We hear the noise from the featureless mass around them,
But the dusk divides. Finality seems to have come.
Nothing can happen now. The attention drifts.
There's a pause; I become a separate thing again,
Almost forget the game, forget my neighbours,
And the noise fades in my ears to a dim rumour.
I watch the lines and colours of field and buildings,
So simple and soft and few in the vapoury air,

135

I am held by the brightening orange lights of the matches
Perpetually pricking the haze across the ground,
And the scene is tinged with a quiet melancholy,
The harmonious sadness of twilight on willowed waters,
Still avenues or harbours seen from the sea.
Yet a louder shout recalls me, I wake again,
Find there are two minutes left; and it's nearly over,
See a few weaklings already walking out,
Caring more to avoid a crush with the crowd
Than to give the last stroke to a ritual of courtesy
And a work of intangible art. But we're all getting ready,
Hope gone, and fear, except in the battling teams.
Regret... a quick movement of hazy forms,
O quiet, O look, there is something happening,
Sudden one phantom form on the other wing
Emerges from nothingness, is singled out,
Curving in a long sweep like a flying gull,
Through the thick fog, swifter as borne by wind,
Swerves at the place where the corner-flag must be,
And runs, by Heaven he's over! and runs, and runs,
And our hearts leap, and our sticks go up in the air
And our hats whirl, and we lose ourselves in a yell
For a try behind the posts. We have beaten them!

Kit Wright

The Burden of the Mystery

It's a strange afternoon's rugby, one player
To a couple of teams of referees,
For the dead outnumber the living
By thirty to one.

That's thirty slow shadow dancers
Round a lit candle,

That's the radiating hub of a many-spoked wheel
And the stamen in the corolla's heart
That forms the inflorescence.

The small craft ploughing toward the harbour lights.

Andy Croft

from *Great North*

Mile Three

"Good heavens, Mardonius, what kind are these that you have pitted us against? It is not for money that they contend, but for glory of achievement!" Herodotus

Mile two-to-three's a young, heroic time;
  The distance yet to run is still compelling
As you begin to slowly, slowly, climb
  Towards the Park Lane roundabout and Felling.
Your legs are pumping well, both feet OK,
  That twinge in your left knee has disappeared,
You feel like you could keep this up all day,
  And now at last the road in front has cleared
Enough at least to try to up the pace,
  Enjoy the sense of movement while you can,
To greet the welcome breeze that's in your face,
  And think this run is going to run to plan.
You pass the garage forecourts' polished cars,
  An old man on his way back from the shops
Who stares at us as if we've come from Mars,
  The kids in black and white Newcastle tops.
Past Gateshead Stadium floodlights' silhouettes
  You feel you could be running in Olympia,
Past javelin field, the shot and discus nets —
  Except their running kit was rather skimpier,
And while they ran in honour of Apollo,
  The god of medicine, back in rocky Delphi,
We honour *private* medicine — hard to swallow
  For those who don't think health's just for the wealthy.

This strange desire to run and run and run
  Belongs to some long centuries-dead Greek farmer;
If you think distance-running's not much fun
  You should try running round in heavy armour!
To run 800m round a field
  Beneath all that implied that you were fit —
That's 60 pounds of helmet, greaves and shield
  (Just like those three Green Howards in full kit).
In Elis, 30,000-plus spectators
  Cheered on their favourites through the olive trees,
Until those breathless, track-side commentators
  Like Pindar, Ceos or Bacchylides
Immediately upon the run's completion
  Immortalised the *victores ludorum*,
Their back-page poems and songs (*viz* Epinician)
  Enable us who never even saw 'em
To feel we've shared the brief athletic pride
  Of runners like the young Hippokleas,
Or three-times lucky Xenophon, who died
  Four hundred years BC. Though runners pass,
The race you run is never really done,
  As in a relay race where each can hear
Beneath your racing heart-beat as you run
  The sound of long dead footsteps drawing near.

How deep this running runs in mortal hearts!
  The human race is one long-running story;
The point we know ourselves as human starts
  When running's not for food, but fame and glory.
As verse defies extinction's cold, dark claims
  In books where long-dead lives may still be read,
So running first began as funeral games,
  At which the quick would entertain the dead.
Both poetry and running's done in metres,
  Both measure out their rhythmed pulse in feet;
You do not have to be as fast as cheetahs
  Or published with the public-school elite,

You don't have to be clever, wise or witty,
  Good looks are no more help than lots of dosh,
You won't run better just because you're pretty
  Or be a better writer if you're posh.
As verse and running both are death-denying,
  They're also both a democratic art
Which anyone can try this side of dying;
  You only need be human to take part.
Mortality is just a lame excuse
  (Just like that painful throb in your left knee)
To please Poseidon or suck up to Zeus.
  On which heroic note you reach mile three.

Mile Twelve

"They shall run and not be weary"
Isaiah

The road climbs Marsden Hill towards the pub
 Where mid-day drinkers guzzle in the sun
And gorge themselves on plates of Sunday grub,
 While you're supposed to get on with the run!
Like thirsty Tantalus the nearness heightens
 Your sense that you'd could drink the North Sea dry,
This kind of torture Zeus reserved for Titans
 Or those so bad they weren't allowed to die,
Like Ixion upon the turning rack,
 Or liverish Prometheus on the rocks,
Like Atlas with the world upon his back,
 Or Sisyphus in vest and running socks.
And yet those tortured creatures were survivors,
 They did not have the option of defeat;
There's something in the taste of old salivas,
 That keeps you running even when you're beat;
Between desire, exhaustion and despair
 Is something more than fresh testosterone;
The world's not made from what we've left to spare
 When we have met the needs of flesh and bone,
We make ourselves with every step we take
 And what we make ourselves this world becomes;
And art is more than icing on the cake,
 (Although arts-funding usually gets the crumbs).

Here art for all is more than distant rumours,
 It isn't just a slogan used by funders;
Like running, it's for doers not consumers,
 Who given half a chance come up with wonders.
Along Prince Edward Road there's cooling waters,
 There's kids with hands held out for you to slap,
Old ladies well supplied with orange quarters,
 And folk to hose you down, or just to clap.
And thanks to Northern Arts and super-Nova
 We run this year to string quartets and jazz,
A carnival to dance to when it's over,
 Millennial (but Dome-less) razzmatazz;
This year the route is lined with flags and banners
 To warm us on a cold October day,
There's 20,000 folk to sing Hosannas,
 And bands to entertain us on the way,
There's drummers, indie combos, bag-pipes, blues,
 And poetry from schools that line the route
There's tableaux, bill-boards, papier-mâché shoes,
 Balloons, cartoons and tunes that constitute
A festival of sound and colour made
 By hundreds of beginners, pros and amateurs,
With art of every shape and every shade
 (Including these iambic-ish pentameters!)

Of all the arts the need to write run's deepest,
 An impulse that all runners understand,
(In funding terms it's certainly the cheapest)
 To leave some mark, some footprints in the sand.
You might expect that in this age of masses —
 Mass culture, media, literacy and sports —
There'd be more athletes from the writing classes,
 More poets dressed in vest and running shorts.
If writing verse resembled losing calories,
 Slim volumes wouldn't seem so limp and tired,
And poets who enjoy the plumpest salaries
 Would not be those who seem the least inspired.
It's said that Philip Larkin kept in trim
 By exercising on his mountain bike,
While T.S. Eliot worked out in the gym,
 And Wordsworth liked to run up Scafell Pike;
John Betjeman was into steeple-chasing;
 And Ted Hughes used to do the Iron Man,
The Martian poets are good at three-legged racing,
 Howay the lads! Just watch those poets gan!
Though some might think the parallel is tenuous,
 The best art's made, like any sport, from sweat,
Like running, it's as pointless as it's strenuous,
 (And this must be as pointless as you get!)

David Duncombe

Going for Silver

400 Metres Final

He knew he wouldn't win, but crouched
to thumb the same line as the champion,
bowing beneath the starter's gun,
a last pretence to be on level terms.

He aimed below the stars, while the man
in golden shoes stretched in the inside lane,
launched into that high-stepping orbit,
head up, catching the sun's salute.

He ran an intelligent race, paced
himself against the also-rans,
surging to finish second in the whole world,
gathering the sweet-enough fruits

within his reach, with still the chance
that the best would shake down,
that the unbeatable would crack
straining for a hundredth of a statistic.

Who then, was the hero? Did the champion need
pursuers, or could he have circled alone?
Would he have sprung so urgently against
the clock? Would a part of a second

be marvellous if we never saw the gap?
Well if it isn't the winning (you've heard
all this) that matters, let's have a biggish hand
for the runner-up. Who, by the way, was third?

Douglas Dunn

Runners

Your skin is whiter, and as you bend fat tells
Your eight years of less than Spartan marriage.
Any man can see what you have been, your legs
That too much sitting cannot discompose,
And synthesis of all movement, your running.
Men still remember you, on the last lap
Of your favourite distance, commander of championships.

Today through the hilly wood, we knew only
Lack of ease, the detritus of beauty
Left to athletes who betray their rule,
A longing of mind for its body, in which
There is no pride, or applause, and whisky
Comes back through months working against us,
The woods are smoke-filled rooms, but no one dare stop.

Douglas Dunn

"In Ten Seconds"

In ten seconds you cannot, as marathoners do,
Think of your family, your hours of training
And everyone you know who has hopes of you.
That happens before in the nights of waiting,
Nights without sleep, or dreaming that you win,
Or dreaming that you lose, waking in sweat —
Dreams rising from your fired adrenalin —
A race you've seen which has not happened yet.
And you long to know, one way or another,
Who of all men is truly the fastest man.
In the important things, he is my brother —
In this, I'll make him look an also ran.

Hamish Henderson

Heroic Song for the Runners of Cyrene
(to Gregorio Prieto)

Without suffering and death one learns nothing.
We should not know the difference between the visions of
the intellect and the facts.
Only those ideas are acceptable that hold through
suffering and death...
Life is that which leaps.
Denis Saurat, "Death and the Dreamer."

I

The runners who would challenge
    the rough bounds of the desert
and strip for the test
    on this barbarous arena
must have sinews like hounds
    and be cunning as jerboas.

Rooting crowds 'll not hail them
    in boisterous circus
nor sleek fame crown their exploit
    with triumph and obelisk.
Sún beats their path
    down the hours of blank silence:
each knows that in the end
    he'll be lucky to have respite.

Freely they'll run
    to the chosen assignation;
ineluctable role,
    and they ready to accept it!
Going with élan of pride
    to the furious onset
they'll reclaim the dead land
    for their city of Cyrene.

Sún beats their path:
    this no course measured plainly
between markers on the beach,
    no event for the novice.
The gates open: are closed.
    And the track leads them forward
hard by salt-lake and standing stone
    blind as the cyclops.

While keeping the same pace
    neither slower nor faster
but as yet out of sight
    behind plateau and escarpment
is history the doppelgaenger
    running to meet them.

II

Stroke of the sun means the hour that's to lay them
is present once more on the dust-blurred horizon.
They start, and awake from their stupor of rhythm —
and think, as they catch glimpse of sea beyond
    watch-tower
they cannot be far from... a place they'd forgotten.

At last it is sure. O, they know that they'll never
be hesitant feet on the marches of darkness
or humped epigonoi, outliving the Fians.

148

No matter what hand stirs the dust, questions gently
with curious touch the grazed stones of the city
yon stroke of the sun vaunts their exploit for ever.

They quicken their pace. (And those others too.) Faster,
and livelier now than at jousts of the Toppo.
The goal is in sight. Simultaneous the onrush,
the clash close at hand, o incarnate dialectic!

The runners gain speed. As they hail their opponents
they can hear in the air the strum of loud arrows
which predestined sing to their point of intersection.
Blaze of harsh day stuns their human defiance;
steel beats their path with its pendulum brilliance.

Sun's thong is lifted. And history the other
emerges at last from the heat's trembling mirror.

III

    Their ruin upon them
they've entered the lip of the burning enclosure.
Each runs to achieve, without pause or evasion
    his instant of nothing

    they look for an opening
grip, grapple, jerk, sway
and fall locking like lovers

down the thunderous cataract of day.

Cyrene, 1942 — Carradale, Argyll, 1947.

149

Roger McGough

Cousin Caroline

Cousin Caroline
was a very fine
sprinter. In the winter
of 1988, with a
bandaged knee
she ran the 100
metres in 10.3

But her best time
was in the dressing room afterwards.

Pascale Petit

Portrait of My Brother as an Endurance Runner

Now that I know the secrets
of the Tarahumara tribe
famous for their long-distance races,
I urge my brother not to eat
Mother's fatty meals. Instead
I feed him rabbits, deer, rats.
Then mix the blood of a turtle
with the blood of a bat
and roll it with tobacco
into a cigar for him to smoke.
I dress him in loose clothes,
dry the head of an eagle
for a charm around his neck,
hang deer-hoof rattles from his waist.
Before Mother stirs, he sets out
at a steady pace, not fast
at first, but never slowing,
until he's run forty miles
in six hours. And so he continues,
the rattlers keep him awake.
Strips of mountain lion skin
protect his ankles.
When night falls, torches
of resinous pinewood are lit
and held by strangers
along the steep forest path.
He keeps on running until
he's old enough to realise
it's better to live in a cave
up a deep canyon alone
than to stay in his mother's house.

Charles Sorley

The Song of the Ungirt Runners

We swing ungirded hips,
And lightened are our eyes,
The rain is on our lips,
We do not run for prize.
We know not whom we trust
Nor whitherward we fare,
But we run because we must
Through the great wide air.

The waters of the seas
Are troubled as by storm.
The tempest strips the trees
And does not leave them warm.
Does the tearing tempest pause?
Do the tree-tops ask it why?
So we run without a cause
'Neath the big bare sky.

The rain is on our lips,
We do not run for prize.
But the storm the water whips
And the wave howls to the skies.
The winds arise and strike it
And scatter it like sand,
And we run because we like it
Through the broad bright land.

Mike Barlow

Offshore with Edward Hopper

There's a stiff breeze at our backs. We're tacking
north west on a steady swell, keeled over
with a fast sea washing the leeward deck.
Now and then the tiller bucks, our wake
a creamy scar healing as it slips away.
From the cockpit I lean out, look upwards
to a lantern of sun scooped in the sail.
If I duck I see land beneath the boom,
a house, white balcony, a figure watching
— us perhaps: the yachtsman and his crew
squinting at dark trees massed behind the house
like a future whose events do not
include them, their small boat bouncing in spray,
the slap of halyards, the creak of stays.
We could just keep sailing, right off the picture
I shout. My quiet companion smiles and nods.
Already there's a bell. We're at the buoy.
Wordlessly we move, prepare to go about.

Helen Dunmore

The Sea Skater

A skater comes to this blue pond,
his worn Canadian skates
held by the straps.

He sits on the grass
lacing stiff boots
into a wreath of effort and breath.

He tugs at the straps and they sound
as ice does when weight troubles it
and cracks bloom around stones

creaking in quiet mid-winter
mid-afternoons: a fine time for a skater.
He knows it and gauges the sun
to see how long it will be safe to skate.

Now he hisses and spins in jumps
while powder ice clings to the air
but by trade he's a long-haul skater.

Little villages, stick-like in the cold,
offer a child or a farm-worker
going his round. These watch him
go beating onward between iced alders
seawards, and so they picture him
always smoothly facing forward, foodless and waterless,
mounting the crusted waves on his skates.

Jane Griffiths

The Skater

Quick against the dead
of landscape, a fluster
of movement with at its edges
hesitancy.

There's a fresh element
this winter: the water's
new solidity, which draws
an expectant cluster

of spectators, and one
in black, who pulls away
without effort, his track
long and powdery

parallels, cross-hatching.
And quick — such surety
in motion it's a vanishing
trick of the light,

as against the sun
between shoulder-high banks
his figure dwindles
across a country that's dark

and barely charted but
by the skates' straight lines
of passage. A territory
where fish show amber in ice,

their eyes unblinking under
the imprint of skates and sky,
roundly containing them:
curved and in miniature.

Susan Wicks

On the Lake

My daughter walks on water.
Quick blades beating, she scuds
across blue distance, gold
anorak plumped by the wind.
Then, flat on her back, she laughs
at the sky, the horizon, the water
under her shot with bubbles.

Now I am just good enough
to pass over her, bend
my stiff arms into wings, scoop
her from the frozen surface.
Our old skates jump grooves, powder
loose ice-fragments, carry us
from one shore to the other.

David Duncombe

Skittleball Goalkeeper

This was the ideal sport for short players
who couldn't aspire to lope along and leap
impossibly high, but scuttled around
slapping the ball at a frantic bounce,
aiming frequently but low, at the pin
in a circle guarded by the keeper.
If the game had caught on, I might still
be signing autographs and commenting
on the lack of skill in the modern game.

It was somehow ignored by the Olympics,
never left the school gymnasium, or I
might have guarded skittle for England,
with Puma and Nike pleading to design
shoes for my nippy sideways crab-shift
and my famous flea-springs over the pin.
My bantamweight frame was perfect, balanced
on slightly bowed legs, just long enough
to step over the pin without toppling it.

I bent and skipped, knees, elbows and fists
to the ball, rebound after rebound
until I caught it and savoured the shouts
of "Me! Me!" before feeding the attack.
Once I knew my worth, I never thought
of playing outside the ring, to cut free,
jink and dodge and angle spectacular shots.
So I stayed where I was, content to wait
for the action. Then you should have seen me.

Sheenagh Pugh

Mozart Playing Billiards

Wolfie drifting round the table
so casual; he had a rhythm,
you know, that cue was part of his arm.
I don't suppose he was even in here
that often, but he was the kind they all
watch: such a sweet mover.

He could have been great: I told him so,
only his heart was never in it.
Playing just relaxed him, helped him write.
You'd see him cock an ear to the click
of the balls, then he'd grab a cue
and tap out tunes, for God's sake.

Catchy tunes, too; folk hummed them
all round town: he had class, Wolfie,
whatever he did... Well, I tell a lie,
there was one thing. That man,
I swear, had the foulest mouth on him.
I'd have to insist, every so often,

please, Wolfie, less of the effing.
Odd, isn't it? Give him a harpsichord
or a cue, he was magic, yet every word
was an embarrassment. Well, there you are,
a man can't be good at everything.
...God, though, he could have been a player.

Jane Holland

Baize Queens

We know this is not life.
Life does not have these corners
cut to pockets on the baize.

We take it oh so seriously though.
We fight to put the black away.
This is not life

but it's as near as dammit
when the green's running smooth
as silk and you're thirty points ahead.

This is not big money, no.
Not for women anyhow,
but still we do it all for love

or so they like to tell us.
This is our battleground.
Like Amazons,

we'd cut our tits off just to win.
We bitch in bathrooms
at the interval

and have our fill
of men who pat our heads
and pat our bums

and show us how to screw
or hold the cue
and ram it up their arses

if we're lucky.
Still, it's just a game.
Always shake her hand

and never cheat. Well played.
That last black really wiped its feet.
Give me a broom

I'll clear the bloody table.
This may not be life
but it's as near as dammit, girls.

David Jacobs

Snooker Players

They dip their cues across the baize, like angling,
Or using geiger counters in a search for minerals.
They line up shots like squinting through a hole.
They cue with the sudden thrusting of harpooning fish.

Immaculately styled hair and tailored evening wear.
Shoes gleam, unnaturally, as if electrically charged.
They progress around the table like hungry lions.
A scratch, scratch scratching as the tip is chalked.

In cubicles, they concentrate on cue and hands,
Using a cloth, like they were working to the bone.
They fuss about the balls, and will not play
Until convinced of surfaces as pure as molecules.

Lawrence Sail

Snooker Players

They whistle the fine smoke
Of blue dust from the cue,
Suave as gunslingers, never
Twitching one muscle too few.
At ease, holstering their thumbs
In trimmest waistcoats, they await
Their opponent's slip, the easiest
of shots miscalculated.
Their sleek heads shine, spangled
With the sure knowledge of every angle.

Once at the table, they bend
In level reverence to squint
At globe after globe, each
With its window of light glinting
On cushioned greener than green,
The rounded image of reason.
One click and cosmology thrives,
All colours know their seasons
And tenderly God in white gloves
Retrieves each fallen planet with love.

Watching them, who could believe
In the world's lack of balance?
Tucked in this pocket of light
Everything seems to make sense —
Where grace is an endless break
And justice, skill repaid,
And all eclipses are merely
A heavenly snooker displayed.
Yet all around, in the framing
Darkness, doubt dogs the game.

162

Alan Bold

The Swimmer

He clings to the water, cleaves
It to him then kicks and shoves
The wet around him, heaves
His chest and shoulders, moves
Into an old dimension.
His instincts take over,
He achieves suspension
In a space full of forever,
A place familiar as a stone's splash
Into a running river
Or a wave's cautious crash
On the edge
Of a sunset-sucking ocean.
Now he's in another age,
Blows bubbles underwater
And watches the air
Take a shine to itself, so clear
It seems to clean the atmosphere.
He shakes himself, lashes out
And presses on
Now that the game's afoot.
He swims, he's having fun
Fancying himself, without a fin,
As a boy becoming dolphin;
Seeing himself take first place
In an inhuman race,
Still, that's a myth,
An aspect of the truth
That hardly touches this liquid moment
That finds him in his element.

Barry Cole

Learning to Swim

This, said my father, at the Tooting Baths
is the deep end. I looked at its green depths
wobbly waves distorting the deep white tiles.

And this, he said, is the shallow end (was
there scorn in his voice?). It, too, was green, but
close up, like a bathroom mirror. Of course I

jumped into the former, my fists banging
the chlorinated water, my legs flap-
flapping, all of me swimming for my life.

Sue Dymoke

Swimmingly

The precocious swimmers
are dipping and weaving,
perfecting their underwater headstands,
their perfect front crawl.
Loving parents look on,
checking each practised stroke,
each kick and turn
as they thread themselves through silken water,
otherworldly.

Never big swimmers in my family.
No history of costumes.
Dad's Egyptian swimming trunks
the only pair handed down.
No Speedo slick slithering
through our photo albums.
Our goggles filled with water,
straps snapped back
leaving ruched marks on shivering chins.

Mrs. Gay was no help,
strutting poolside in dipped white stilettos,
pulling tight the rip cord of her short shiny mac.
Swimming teacher, rainwear model extraordinaire,
water was her fashion accessory.

She didn't feel the chlorine bubbling up our noses
as we struggled to complete a single length,
without touching the bottom,
without gripping the sides,
didn't understand our fear of cramp,
damp, evil liquid covering our heads,
coating our limbs.

And still they swim past us forever,
through all those school galas,
"fun" days at the pool.
Those quick confident bodies,
eyes shining,
hair a permanent wave.
They make their own waterways,
skimming like smoothed stones,
leaving us behind:
an embarrassment of puddles,
muddled hands flapping
at the mysterious blue.

Vicki Feaver

Swimming in January

Because, like every new lover,
I want to enter the underworld
and take you with me, I lead you
into the sea in January — naked into a sea
that flows round our calves and knees
like green fire: deeper and deeper —
feet off the shingle now — gulping half air,
half salt-water, drifting almost to the edge
where there's no returning
before we strike back
to the beach — past windsurfers
sealed in rubber wet-suits, struggling
to lift orange sails, past wading birds
dipping yellow beaks into a film
of mirrored cloud — emerge,
white legs moving like sticks over
oil-blackened sand, at the breakwater
where we draped clothes and towels,
rubbing each other back to life.

Pamela Gillilan

The Half-mile

I was twelve when I swam the half-mile,
up and down the tide-fed cold concrete
pool, with a slow steady side-stroke.
My father counted the lengths,
at first from the deep-end board
and then, as I moved more laboriously,
pacing alongside, urging me on.

The race was only against myself
and distance. The grainy salt water,
though not translucent like the chlorinated
blue lidos of town, buoyed me helpfully,
lapped softly against the bath's grey sides
variegated with embedded hardcore pebbles.
I swam from goal to alternate goal; he counted.

When he called enough I scrambled
over the sharp shutter-cast lip,
shuddered into a dry towel, drank
the words of praise. The planks
of the changing-room walls
were warm to touch. It had seemed to be
a great deal of swimming; still does.

James Kirkup

Synchronised Swimming

Attach butterfly nose-clips —
ladylike gentility
  will never lose points —
then march, a female army
  of varying heights

but all with fixed dentition
in waterproof rouge simpers
  with the Red Army's
bravely-lifted chins — eyes right!
  Salute the host's flag!

After lining up one by
one, in battle order, you
  launch off sideways, one
by one, octuplet splash of
  floral plastic caps.

Only to re-surface in
tight formation, but all smiles,
  as if getting wet
was nothing, submerging with
  beauty parade chic.

Underwater chin-waggings
produce a rose window of
  expanding blossoms.
Dives are perpendicular
  plunges — never show

your bottoms to the public —
tops lifted high but not dry
  out of the deep end
by rising pyramids of
  cute water-pixies

that become ever-changing
kaleidoscopic patterns —
  dinky toes, fluttered
fairy fingers, shaven legs —
  broad-shouldered sirens

seem to be waving helpless
arms before going under —
  not for the last time —
they are waving not drowning —
  hold the lifeboat crews!

The wheels of carnival carts,
clock faces telling no time
  dissolving into
cat's cradle squares, triangles,
  pretty polygons.

The number eight does not leave
much room for manoeuvring —
  doubly four-cornered
figures, always fatally
  end up in a line

that to the strident strains
of the Colonel Bogey march must
  trudge back to the brink —
smiling through the tears (they've lost!)
  and butterfly nose-clips.

Jean Sprackland

Synchronised Drowning

When I give the signal
the glamour begins.
Let the cold curtain
fold over you.
Tread the space heavily
and beat a froth with your arms.
You can be confident
that my movements are mirroring yours.
Open your mouth on water
slick with small jelly life;
feel your tongue swimming
with microscopic fear.
The important thing is precision
and a bright smile.
Open your lungs
and breathe green air
stranded with weed.
Relax. After all that practice
our timing is bound to be good.
Let the mud floor tug you.
Take a last look at sunlight
streaking the oily surface above.
Roll your eyes and sing with me
a steady diminuendo of bubbles.

Gareth Owen

Ping-Pong

Swatted between bats
The celluloid ball
Leaps on unseen elastic
Skimming the taut net.

Sliced		Spun
Screwed		Cut
Dabbed		Smashed
	Point	
	Service	
Ping		Pong
Pong		Ping
Bing		Bong
Bong		Bing
	Point	
	Service	
Ding		Dong
Dong		Ding
Ting		Tong
Tang		Tong
	Point	
	Service	
Angled		Slipped
Cut		Driven
Floated		Caressed
Driven		Hammered

THWACKED
Point

	Service	
Bit		Bat
Tip		Tap
Slip		Slap
Zip		Zap
Whip		Whap
	Point	
	Service	
Left		Yes
Right		Yes
Twist		Yes
Skids		Yes
Eighteen		Seventeen
Eighteen		All
Nineteen		Eighteen
Nineteen		All
Twenty		Nineteen
	Point	
	Service	
Forehand		Backhand
Swerves		Yes
Rockets		Yes
Battered		Ah
Cracked		Ah
	Smashed	

Smashed

SMASHED

GAME

Mandy Coe

Ten Pin

As the girls puff up their cheeks
and blow out smoke, they look
like woodcuts of the wind
cornered on maps of a mediaeval world.
But their continent is tiny, car park
and bowling alley. Its sea,
a puddle where mythical beasts
are reflected in red neon curves.

Colossus — the bouncer — straddles
the entrance. Behind him is the clatter
of coins, harsh bursts of song:
plum, plum, golden bell;
bar, bar, plum.
Deeper in the gloom
comes the rolling roar of wood on wood,
the axe-strike shriek of human glee.

Figures in a nativity scene, white skittles
await each player's eye and aim.
The heartbeat pause of ball, offered up
as a votive gift, then the step, dip and swing.
Soft shoes whisper as bowlers skip back.
For everyone knows the tumbling darkness
conceals the edge of the world.

John Betjeman

A Subaltern's Love-song

Miss J. Hunter Dunn, Miss J. Hunter Dunn,
Furnish'd and burnish'd by Aldershot sun,
What strenuous singles we played after tea,
We in the tournament — you against me!

Love-thirty, love-forty, oh! weakness of joy,
The speed of a swallow, the grace of a boy,
With carefullest carelessness, gaily you won,
I am weak from your loveliness, Joan Hunter Dunn.

Miss Joan Hunter Dunn, Miss Joan Hunter Dunn,
How mad I am, sad I am, glad that you won.
The warm-handled racket is back in its press,
But my shock-headed victor, she loves me no less.

Her father's euonymus shines as we walk,
And swing past the summer-house, buried in talk,
And cool the verandah that welcomes us in
To the six-o'clock news and a lime-juice and gin.

The scent of the conifers, sound of the bath,
The view from my bedroom of moss-dappled path,
As I struggle with double-end evening tie,
For we dance at the Golf Club, my victor and I.

On the floor of her bedroom lie blazer and shorts
And the cream-coloured walls are be-trophied with sports,
And westering, questioning settles the sun
On your low-leaded window, Miss Joan Hunter Dunn.

The Hillman is waiting, the light's in the hall,
The pictures of Egypt are bright on the wall,
My sweet, I am standing beside the oak stair
And there on the landing's the light on your hair.

By roads "not adopted", by woodlanded ways,
She drove to the club in the late summer haze,
Into nine-o'clock Camberley, heavy with bells
And mushroomy, pine-woody, evergreen smells.

Miss Joan Hunter Dunn, Miss Joan Hunter Dunn,
I can hear from the car-park the dance has begun.
Oh! full Surrey twilight! importunate band!
Oh! strongly adorable tennis-girl's hand!

Around us are Rovers and Austins afar,
Above us, the intimate roof of the car,
And here on my right is the girl of my choice,
With the tilt of her nose and the chime of her voice,

And the scent of her wrap, and the words never said,
And the ominous, ominous dancing ahead.
We sat in the car park till twenty to one
And now I'm engaged to Miss Joan Hunter Dunn.

Roger McGough

40–   *Love*

middle	aged
couple	playing
ten	nis
when	the
game	ends
and	they
go	home
the	net
will	still
be	be
tween	them

Ian McMillan

The Tennis Ball Poem

1.
Everywhere the lines; the balls.
Long, long fluorescent lights.
By the coffee machine, the restless
attempts for change in purses.
The enormous laughing women, there,
and the men studying the back pages.
Everywhere the lines. The balls
falling in lines from the broken
conveyor, landing on the greased
head of a man in a white coat.
Early in the evening at the bottom
of the gently sloping ramp a boy
tackles me about crossword puzzles.
Everywhere the lines, the balls.

2.
The manager who is about to go insane
holds up to me in the early hours
of a hot morning in Summer

a piece of rubber and a massive spider.
"Still alive" he says. "Still alive Mac."

Later, in the canteen, I tell George.
He mishears me: "Aye, Mac, we're just
grovelling in the bastard dust, just
crawling in the bastard dust."

And somewhere, just, the spider
is still alive in the night sky.

178

3.
The accumulated straightness of it all.
Huge steel straightness within which
Charlie sells pens, birthday cards, chocolate.

Why are the wicked so strong?

Not you, Charlie, not you;
sell me your goods.

4.
A dog peeps into the noisy room.
The manager who will go insane
puts on his dog-in-the-factory face
and calls a meaningless name
into the bouncing air.

Later he will forget this. Later
I remember his face
as he spoke to the dog's indifference.

5.
The two women are fighting
near the office. Some workers
notice, some see nothing.

The fight is short, vicious,
loud, uncontrolled, full
of itself and its ramifications.

Until one of them is locked
in the office and the other
runs home, they are fighting.

A future, a new order.
A struggle, nothing to go on,
the harsh lights, shadows.

A future composed simply
of the present. Men running
against angular, clicking

machines to a fight.

6.
Talk to me without moving your
lips; without inviting any doors
to pop open, sell me your

unfortunate tendency to
speak, speak or to fall
silent. Upstairs, I dress.

"You call this a life?"
shouts Albert the Fitter
looking down at my hair

from his enormous height,
and I say something small,
negative, about seeing,

waiting. Albert and the back
of his long RAF neck
lean into the machine,

applying grease. Upstairs
I take positive steps.

7.
The telephone rings at five o'clock in the morning.
No-one in the canteen
moves. We have lost our bastard hands.

Dunlop Sports Company, Feb 1980–May 1981

Lawrence Sail

Fives Courts

for Matthew

In every place the courts were set apart,
hidden behind the armoury or the bike sheds,
a good place for a quick grope or a gasper.
Empty, they seemed banal as a torturer's cellar:
a row of sties that didn't smell quite right.

Blank walls, a toy door, four large lights
in metal shades with grilles, shining onto
slabbed stone. Along the front, a bar
of wood. In autumn, the courts streamed with wet:
in winter, the wind drove snow across the thresholds.

In an old biscuit tin, a selection of gloves
limp as exhausted fish; Slazengers, the colour
of dried blood, Grasshoppers a dull grey.
In most, the fingers unstitched, the padding lumpy:
in all, an ingrained smell of stale sweat.

Only the ball was intricate. On old ones,
like mad surgery, little spiralling lines
of red stitches pulled the cover tight
around a core of rubber, cotton and cork.
Nowadays they just glue the seams into place.

The play's the thing, pure ingenuity —
the crack of a service rocketing out from the corner,
the ball hammered off the back wall, the sly lob,
the boast that ricochets madly off one or both
side-walls and dies irretrievably by the bar.

Enter the ghost of Hazlitt, himself a player,
who wrote that "poetry puts a spirit of life
and motion into the universe" — and knew
how much depended on the playful imagination,
on keeping warm in the coldest places on earth.

William Scammell

Arms and the Court

Summer pavilions. The cream of the cream
has trickled along to club and court,
lately risen from Lascaux's dream
to the art of geometric thought.

Who is this warrior, in snowy cloth
to freeze his intentions? What ancient race
is pending here, and who is the moth
of a girl who flutters all over the place?

The lyre has crumbled; the lyre's re-strung.
The grass glows like Achilles' shield.
Leaping down off the vase, they've flung
sheer carelessness at the weight of the world.

It's May, or it's June, when the greenery grows
long gawky limbs, and the cars go mad,
everything reeks, there's nothing to lose
but what was lost when the world was made.

They pause for a rest. Unscrewing the flask
they're lounging by the Lydian spring,
unbuttoned, still chasing after a wish
    and a brown arm flashing.

William Scammell

Golden Dawn

A backhand slice is but a paltry shot,
no backbone in it, *sauve qui peut*, unless
hit to the corner baseline, asymptote
plus foxy coda, underspun duress
allowing one to charge in, *tête-à-tête*,
and do a hotshot number at the net.

When I was young and skinny, I'd not weight
enough to terrorise the baldest ball.
Now that I'm thick, and wise, and forty-eight
and compact of the waist chimerical
the drop-shot wounds me, and the high lob pains.
Either the body's lacking, or the brains,

it's never damn well right. And that's a shame.
O sages in your manuals, Kenny, Fred,
come be the singing-masters of my game,
that ace-tormented serve, weak overhead!
Iron out my faults. Let these joints thrive
and put some bottle in my cross-court drive!

Once in the rankings I shall never smoke
or swear, raise hell at discos, quarrel, swank.
If I can have a swimming pool, and poke
my troubles in the eye, break the odd bank,
I'll bow out gracefully, by fame paroled,
and sit up in the stands as good as gold.

William Scammell

John McEnroe

All Britain's deepest fears about spoilt brats
were thrillingly confirmed. You were THE PITS
John, an expression new to us. We heard
it as a ripe four-letter word
you'd dropped, splat! on the hallowed umpire's head.
At Wimbledon! Oh boy, but you were bad!
The nation's right arm ached, was overcome
with transcendental lust to smack your bum.
And Irish, too... That baked-potato face,
that fallen-cherub frizz, that verbal mace
you sprayed at linesmen, paparazzi, anyone
who'd got the gall to get their act between
your eye, the ball, your will, the clean
unanswerable line of pure perfection.

Stuffed shirts, stuffed balls, stuffed amateurs,
stuffed Royal Box, stuffed Chelsea Pensioners,
stuffed accents — *Pleeeaay*! — stuffed calls, stuffed
    sniggers, stuff
they know to handle Brooklyn way. Hang tough.

William Scammell

The Tennis Court Oath

I solemnly swear that I shall buy, regardless of cost, the biggest and best and latest break-through in tennis racquet technology not less than four months after its manufacture and launch, in the sure and certain hope that some of its magic will rub off on me, including Chrissie's groundstrokes and Stefan's first volley.

I hereby give assurance that I shall also splash out on the latest in leisurewear, no matter how tasteless the innovative riot of colour on my shirt, the track-suit billowing on my back, the winged contraptions on my feet.

I promise further that I will take out a small mortgage in order to buy new tennis balls, and undertake to turn a blind eye to this annual extortion practised on myself and other members of the British public.

I will endure bad courts, bad weather, amateur coaching, postal tournaments, LTA officials, saturation coverage of Wimbledon and no-TV-tennis-for-the-rest-of-the-year, home counties folie de grandeur, few or no indoor courts except school halls with multiple line-markings, tennis elbow, housemaid's knee, athlete's foot, hammer toes, callouses, tendonitis, server's torque, chronic abrasions of self-esteem, and promise not to complain, ever.

Fleur Adcock

A Game

They are throwing the ball
to and fro between them,
in and out of the picture.
She is in the painting
hung on the wall
in a narrow gold frame.
He stands on the floor
catching and tossing
at the right distance.
She wears a white dress,
black boots and stockings,
and a flowered straw hat.
She moves in silence
but it seems from her face
that she must be laughing.
Behind her is sunlight
and a tree-filled garden;
you might think to hear
birds or running water,
but no, there is nothing.
Once or twice he has spoken
but does so no more,
for she cannot answer.
So he stands smiling,
playing her game
(she is almost a child),
not daring to go,
intent on the ball.
And she is the same.
For what would result
neither wishes to know
if it should fall.

Simon Armitage

Great Sporting Moments: The Treble

The rich! l love them. Trust them to suppose
the gift of tennis is deep in their bones.

Those chaps from the coast with all their own gear
from electric eyes to the umpire's chair,

like him whose arse I whipped with five choice strokes
perfected on West Yorkshire's threadbare courts:

a big first serve that strained his alloy frame,
a straight return that went back like a train,

a lob that left him gawping like a fish,
a backhand pass that kicked and drew a wisp

of chalk, a smash like a rubber bullet
and a bruise to go with it. Three straight sets.

Smarting in the locker rooms he offered
double or quits; he was a born golfer

and round the links he'd wipe the floor with me.
I played the ignoramus to a tee:

the pleb in the gag who asked the viscount
what those eggcup-like things were all about —

"They're to rest my balls on when I'm driving."
"Blimey, guv, Rolls-Royce think of everything" —

but at the fifth when I hadn't faltered
he lost his rag and threw down the gauntlet;

we'd settle this like men: with the gloves on.
I said, no, no, no, no, no, no, no. OK, come on then.

Kate Clanchy

Teams

I would have skipped the stupid games,
long afternoons spent chilled in goal,
or sleepy, scratching, in deep field,
leapt the sagging fence
and learnt, as others do, apparently,
from dying mice, cow parsley,

if it weren't for this persistent sense
of something — like the words to songs,
sung out on the bus
to matches, like my name on lists
on notice boards, shortened
called across the pitch,

trusted by the ones who knew,
the ones with casual shoulders, cool —
that thing, I mean, that knack, that ease,
still sailing, like those hockey balls,
like sodden summer tennis balls,
right past me.

Sue Dymoke

All in a Game

Under starter's orders they wait
to bully off, dive in, kick off
break off, take aim, tee off
tip off, catch the wave, cast off

they're poised for
the throw up, quick start
splashdown

they're ready, they're steady, they get set
the whistle blows, pistol fires,
bleeper sounds, umpire calls

and they serve play run pass
dr
  ib
    bl
      e

and they leap dodge throw sprint
sh   my
  im

and they slide edge swerve hit

                   y
                e
             l
           l
         o
       v

and they drive chip curl bowl

g
o
o
g
l
i
e
s

and they score ace catch smash
b
i
r
d
i
e
(or they FOUL! miss, net, dr
                              op
no ball)

Off piste in the sin bin rough
some are red carded, timed out and taking the
l   o   n   g   w   a   l   k
to an early bath

while the rest go on towards
the eighteenth green
last hurdle
final quarter

the twelfth round
last lap
final metre

the tenth wicket
home straight
final over

191

the match point
golden goal
clear water

On and on and on to
the chequered flag,
close of play
when they'll relive
the sweat, grief and tears
joy, hope and fears
missed chances
backward glances
the 90 minutes, 11 wickets
2 halves, 3 sets
worth of defeat or glory
of pleasure or pain
their side of each game's story
replay it all over again

Sue Dymoke

Games before Tea

A thousand eyes swirl across the green.
Ali Babas, albinos and chinamen
opalescent colours pour from fine lattice bags,
pulled tight with drawstrings
to stop out the sun.

Coaxed and fussed over
the marbles roll
their owners whispering prayers of protection
against each chip, each slithered edge
as a ball bearing glints.

The best seldom appear:
the small pearly blue;
the colourless ones of unusual shape and size
stay deep inside
safe since their rescue from a cough sweet tin
half hidden at the back of Gran's cupboard.

These are the security,
precious reserve when
game after game slips away.
In the long minutes before tea
one must go out in a sparkle of light.

Spike Hawkins

The Five to Six Results

hurt results away
north ground flames
at home
matchplay to torture
in nets old bridgford
showed a leg in coming
events
sanctuary nil

Roger McGough

Uncle Jed

Uncle Jed
Durham bred
raced pigeons
for money.

He died
a poor man
however

as the pigeons
were invariably
too quick for him.

195

Roger McGough

Uncle Philip

Uncle Philip was hopeless at waterpolo
it just wasn't the game for him
for starters he was colourblind
and besides he couldn't swim.

Banned from English swimming pools
for disobeying basic rules
he emigrated to Eire
where officials were fairer.

From Donegal to Bantry Bay
audiences he astounded
until one fateful Galway day
when his polopony drownded.

Ian McMillan

Three Boring Miles on the Exercise Bike

Three boring miles. The television flickering
in the corner of my eye. A man talking.

The view doesn't alter, of course. The rain
coming down steadily, Joe's grandma

taking him down to school, coming back again.
Mile one. The speedometer hovering

around twelve. So in an hour I could be
almost in Sheffield, halfway to Leeds,

my legs going slowly, slowly, going nowhere,
my wife lifting the same cup of coffee

to her lips for mile after mile, the steam
pulling away from the cup like smoke,

a man talking. It's me, saying the same things
over and over again. Mile two. The phone rings,

I pedal, my wife answers it again and again.
It's the same bad news, pulling away like smoke,

Joe's grandma taking him to school.
She waves this time. She waved last time.

Her glasses are the same as they have been for years.
My view doesn't change. A window of trees,

rain, Joe's grandma, my wife, the cup of coffee,
the telephone, the bad news, my legs going slowly,

slowly, in an hour I could be halfway to here,
almost into this room, the room pulling away

like smoke from a dying fire. Mile three.
The view doesn't alter. A man talking. It's me.

Norman MacCaig

Highland Games

They sit on the heather slopes
and stand six deep round the rope ring.
Keepers and shepherds in their best plus-fours
who live mountains apart
exchange gossip and tall stories.
Women hand out sandwiches,
rock prams and exchange
small stories and gossip.
The Chieftain leans his English accent
on a five-foot crook and feels
one of the natives.

The rope ring is full
of strenuous metaphors.
Eight runners shoulder each other
eight times round it — a mile
against the dock that will kill them.
Little girls breasted only with medals translate
a tune that will outlast them
with formalised legs and
antler arms. High jumpers
come down to earth and,
in the centre
a waddling "heavy" tries to throw
the tree of life in one straight line.

Thank God for the bar, thank God
for the Games Night Dance — even though they end
in the long walk home
with people no longer here — with exiles and deaths —
your nearest companions.

199

Jack Mapanje

Skipping Without Ropes

I will, I will skip without your rope
Since you say I should not, I cannot
Borrow your son's skipping rope to
Exercise my limbs, I will skip without

Your rope as you say even the lace
I want will hang my neck until I die
I will create my own rope, my own
Hope and skip without your rope as

You insist I do not require to stretch
My limbs fixed by these fevers of your
Reeking sweat and your prison walls
I will, will skip with my forged hope;

Watch, watch me skip without your
Rope watch me skip with my hope
A-one, a-two, a-three, a-four, a-five
I will, a-seven, I do, will skip, a-ten,

Eleven, I will skip without, will skip
Within and skip I do without your
Rope but with my hope; and I will,
Will always skip you dull, will skip

Your silly rules, skip your filthy walls
Your weevil pigeon peas, skip your
Scorpions, skip your Excellency Life
Glory; I do, you don't, I can, you can't,

I will, you won't, I see, you don't, I
Sweat, you don't, I will, will wipe my
Gluey brow then wipe you at a stroke
I will, will wipe your horrid, stinking,

Vulgar prison rules, will wipe you all
Then hop about, hop about my cell, my
Home, the mountains, my globe as your
Sparrow hops about your prison yard

without your hope, without your rope
I swear, I will skip without your rope, I
Declare, I will have you take me to your
Showers to bathe me where I can resist

This singing child you want to shape me
I'll fight your rope, your rules, your hope
As your sparrow does under your super-
vision! Guards! Take us for the shower!

Sean O'Brien

Dignified
from *Sports Pages*

On grim estates at dawn, on college tracks,
In rings, in wheelchairs, velodromes and pools,
While we snore on towards our heart attacks,
They will outstrip the bullet and the fax,
They will rewrite the body and its rules.

Athletes who amazed Zeus and Apollo,
Rivalling their supernatural ease,
Must make do nowadays with us, who follow,
Breathless, on a billion TVs.
Should we believe it's us they aim to please?

The purpose stays essentially the same:
To do what's difficult because they can,
To sign in gold an ordinary name
Across the air from Georgia to Japan,
To change the world by mastering a game.

The rest of us, left waiting at the start,
Still celebrate, as those the gods adore
Today stake everybody's claims for more
By showing life itself becoming art,
Applauded by a planetary roar —

The gun, the clock, the lens, all testify
That those who win take liberties with time:
The sprinter's bow, the vaulter's farewell climb,
The swimmer who escapes her wake, deny
What all the gods insist on, that we die.

Gael Turnbull

A Racing Walker

If you define what's not unnatural
and persevere in that most strictly
you'll soon cross the frontier
into that single-minded kingdom
where strides a racing walker
who is consumed by the commitment not to...
not to do what would be merely natural —
who makes both mockery of what he doesn't
and veneration of his refusal of the easy answer —
who is the self-mortifying saint of travellers,
ascetic of movement, clown of urgency,
even a sort of hero of the ungainly —
and commands our amazement
by the ferocity of his intransigence.

Biographical Details

Fleur Adcock was born in Auckland, New Zealand and moved to London in the 1960s. A collected edition of Fleur Adcock's poetry, *Poems 1960-2000*, was published by Bloodaxe and she is a regular contributor to poetry anthologies as well as an editor and translator.

Allan Ahlberg has won numerous awards for his children's books such as the Kurt Maschler Award, The Children's Book Award, the Blue Peter Book Award. His poetry collections include *Please Mrs Butler* and *Friendly Matches* (Puffin).

John Arlott was best known as a BBC cricket commentator, however he was also a wine connoisseur, author and poet. His poetry collections include *Of Period and Place* (Cape).

Simon Armitage was born in Huddersfield in 1963. He worked for several years as a probation officer before becoming a full-time writer. He has written two novels, several stage plays and nine books of poetry, including *Zoom!* and *The Universal Home Doctor*. He currently teaches at Manchester Metropolitan University. He supports Manchester United.

Mike Barlow's first collection, *Living on the Difference,* published by Smith/Doorstop, was shortlisted for the 2005 Jerwood Aldeburgh Prize. He is also a visual artist. His recreational time has always involved outdoor pursuits, particularly walking and climbing in the remoter regions of the UK.

James Berry was born in Jamaica in 1924. He has lived in the UK since 1948. He has edited several anthologies of anthologies of Caribbean poetry, and written many books for children and adults including *Hot Earth Cold Earth* and *Only One of Me*. He was awarded the OBE in 1991. He lives in Brighton.

John Betjeman (1906-84) was born in London. He worked for several years as a journalist, writing *Shell Guides* and editing the *Architectural Review*. His many books included *Summoned by Bells, Church Poems* and the best-selling *Collected Poems*. He was awarded the OBE, the CBE, and was knighted in 1969. In 1972 he was appointed Poet Laureate.

Alan Bold (1943-98) was born in Edinburgh. He trained as a journalist, but worked for most of his life as a full-time poet, editor and anthologist. Among his many books are *The Penguin Book of Socialist Verse* and *Poetry in Motion*. His own poetry was featured in *Penguin Modern Poets*.

Jean 'Binta' Breeze is a Jamaican Dub poet and story-teller who performs her work all over the world and divides her time between Leicester and Jamaica. Her collections include *On the Edge of an Island* and *Quadrille* (Bloodaxe).

Adrian Buckner was born in London and studied in Swansea before moving to the Midlands. He is the editor of *Poetry Nottingham* and a seasoned club cricketer whose best season is yet to come.

Kevin Cadwallender has worked as a policeman, a roadie, a clown and poet-in-residence at the Co-op. His books of poetry include *Public* and *Baz Uber Alles*. He lives in Sunderland.

Kate Clanchy was born in Glasgow and now works in Oxford. She is a regular contributor to the *Guardian* and the author of three poetry collections *Slattern*, *Samarkand* and *New Born*.

Brendan Cleary was born in Northern Ireland. A former editor of *Stand* and *The Echo Room*, his books of poetry include *White Bread and ITV*, *The Irish Card* and *Sacrilege*. He currently lives in Brighton.

Mandy Coe is an award winning poet who lives in Liverpool and works extensively on writing in education projects. Her collections are *Pinning the Tail on the Donkey* (Spike) and *The Weight of Cows* (Shoestring Press).

Barry Cole has lived in London for most of his life apart from two years spent as a Northern Arts Fellow in Literature at the universities of Durham and Newcastle-upon-Tyne. He is a freelance editor and writer with four novels and seven collections of poetry, including *Ghosts are People Too* and *Inside Outside: New & Selected Poems* (Shoestring Press).

Stanley Cook (1922-91) was born in Austerfield, South Yorkshire. He taught for many years in Yorkshire schools, later at Huddersfield Polytechnic. His collected poems, *Woods Beyond a Cornfield* were published posthumously.

Wendy Cope read history at Oxford and worked as a primary school teacher before finding success with her first collection *Making Cocoa for Kingsley Amis*. Other collections include *Serious Concerns* and *If I Don't Know* (Faber & Faber).

David Craig was born in Aberdeen in 1932. He taught Creative Writing at the University of Lancaster for many years. His many books include three novels, five books of travel and oral history and four collections of poetry. He lives in Cumbria.

Andy Croft has published six books of poetry, the latest being *Comrade Laughter*, and thirty-four books for teenagers, mostly about football. He was once Poet-in-Residence on the Great North Run. He still plays five-a-side football and is a season-ticket holder at Middlesbrough FC. Together with Adrian Mitchell he edited the Five Leaves' collection *Red Sky at Night: an anthology of socialist poetry*.

Simon Curtis was brought up in Northamptonshire. He taught at the University of Manchester for over twenty years and used to edit the *Thomas Hardy Journal*. His most recent collection of poems is *Reading a River: New and Selected Poems*. He supports Burnley FC.

Camilla Doyle's *A Game of Bowls* was written at the time of air raids on Norwich in April 1942.

Alan Dent teaches modern languages in a comprehensive school in Preston. His most recent books of poetry are *Who* and *Town*. He edits *Penniless Press*, and used to play on the left-wing for Crookings Lane Primary School.

Jeremy Duffield has lived in the East Midlands all his life. He has been chair of Nottingham Poetry Society for over a decade. His first full collection was *Oak Apples and Heavenly Kisses* (Headland).

David Duncombe lives in Matlock, Derbyshire. His drama and stories have been broadcast by the BBC, he has two children's novels published and four poetry collections.

Helen Dunmore is a poet, novelist and children's writer. Her latest novel is *House of Orphans* (Viking, 2006) and a new collection of poems, *Glad of These Times*, will be published in spring 2007 by Bloodaxe Books. She was the inaugural winner of the Orange Prize for Fiction, and is a Fellow of the Royal Society of Literature.

Douglas Dunn was born in Renfrewshire in 1941. He worked for many years as a librarian and is now Professor of English and Director of Scottish Studies at St Andrews University. He has published eight books of poetry, from *Terry Street* to *New Selected Poems 1964-2000*.

Sue Dymoke is the poetry editor of *English in Education*. Her books include *The New Girls* (*New and Selected Poems* published by Shoestring Press) and *Drafting and Assessing Poetry* (Paul Chapman Publishing). She lectures in education at the University of Leicester. She has been an ardent Chelsea FC supporter since the age of ten and is now an enthusiastic, but slow, swimmer.

U.A. Fanthorpe was born in London in 1929. For many years she taught at Cheltenham Ladies College, before leaving to work as a hospital receptionist. She has published many books of poetry, most recently *Queuing for the Sun* and *Collected Poems 1978-2000*. The first woman ever to be nominated as Oxford Professor of Poetry, she has been awarded the Queen's Medal for Poetry and a CBE.

Vicki Feaver was born in Nottingham, studied at Durham and University College London and is now Emeritus Professor at the University of Chichester. She has published three collections: *Close Relatives* (Secker), and *The Handless Maiden* and *The Book of Blood* (both Cape).

Kevin Fegan has written over fifty plays and worked as a storyline writer for *Coronation Street*. He has published seven volumes of poetry and regularly performs his work. Collections include *Racer, Blast* and *Let Your Left Hand Sing,* published by Five Leaves.

Elaine Feinstein is a poet, translator, novelist and biographer of Pushkin, Tsvetayeva and Bessie Smith. Her collections include *Gold, Daylight* and *Selected Poems* (Carcanet).

Linda France was born in Newcastle. She has written for the stage and worked on many Public Art collaborations. She has published five books of poems, most recently *The Simultaneous Dress*, and a verse-biography of Lady Mary Wortley Montagu, *The Toast of the Kit Cat Club*. She lives in Northumberland.

Rosie Garner is a Nottingham poet best known for her Arts Council sponsored project *Poetry on the Buses* – poems for the whole of the Nottingham City Transport Network. Poems have also appeared in magazines and in her pamphlet collection *We're All Here With Our Buttons Done Up Wrong*.

Pamela Gillilan (1918-2001) published her first book of poems at the age of sixty-eight. She was stationed with Bomber Command during the Second World War and later worked in the family furniture-restoring business. Her books included *All Steel Traveller: New and Selected Poems* and *The Rashomon Syndrome*.

Martin Green is a poet and author whose latest published collection is *A Night with Fiona Pitt-Kethley*. For many years he was a publisher, and among his authors were Hugh MacDiarmid and Patrick Kavanagh. For the last thirty years he has lived off and on in Cornwall.

Jane Griffiths was born in Exeter and grew up in Holland. She teaches at the University of Edinburgh. She has published two books of poetry, *A Grip on Thin Air* and *Icarus on Earth*.

Cathy Grindrod is the author of *Fighting Talk* (Headland) and the pamphlet collections *Still Breathing* (Five Leaves) and *Something The Heart Can't Hold*. She is a literature development officer and Poet Laureate for Derbyshire.

Mike Harding was born in Crumpshall, Manchester in 1944. He has worked as a dustman, bus-conductor, carpet-fitter, teacher, folk-musician and poet. His books include *Daddy Edgar's Pools* and *Crystal Set Dreams*. He is a life-time vice-president of the Ramblers Association.

Tony Harrison was born in Leeds in 1937. He has trans-lated, written, and directed many plays for the National Theatre and the RSC, and written several award-winning poems for the screen. His many collections of poems include *Laureate's Block* and *Under the Clock*. He lives in Newcastle.

Spike Hawkins is a veteran of the Liverpool Poets move-ment. He performed at the Poetry Olympics events at the Albert Hall in 1965 and 2005.

Seamus Heaney was born in County Derry, Northern Ireland. His first book, *Death of a Naturalist,* appeared in 1966. He was awarded the Nobel Prize for Literature in 1995 and his latest collection is *District and Circle* (Faber & Faber).

Hamish Henderson (1919-2002) was born in Perthshire. A pioneer of the Scottish Folk Revival in the 1950s and 1960s, he worked for fifty years in the School of Scottish Studies at Edinburgh University. His writings were col-lected before his death in *Collected Poems and Songs* and *Alias MacAlias*.

Selima Hill was born in London in 1945. She has worked on many multimedia projects with the Royal Ballet and the Welsh National Opera. She has written 11 books of poetry, including *Trembling Hearts in the Bodies of Dogs: New and Selected Poems* and her most recent, *Lou-Lou*. She lives in Dorset.

Jane Holland was born in Essex in 1966. She has published a book of poems, *The Brief History of a Disreputable Woman* and a novel, *Kissing the Pink*. She was once 24th in the women's world snooker rankings.

Ian Horn lives in Shotton Colliery, Co. Durham. He has edited an anthology of poems about football *Verses United*, and published a pamphlet *Jazz from the Collieries*. He supports Sunderland FC.

Michael Horovitz is a poet, singer-songwriter, jazz and blues musician, visual artist, editor of *New Departures* and producer of *Poetry Olympics* festivals. He is about to publish *A New Waste Land: Timeship Earth at Nillennium*. More via http//:www.poetryolympics.com.

Ted Hughes (1930-1998) was born in Yorkshire. He was appointed Poet Laureate in 1984. His poetry collections include *The Hawk in the Rain, The Birthday Letters* and *Collected Poems* (Faber & Faber).

David Jacobs was born in London in 1959. His books include *Harlem Road* and *The Gardens of Onkel Arnold*.

Mike Jenkins teaches at a comprehensive school in Merthyr. For many years he edited *Poetry Wales*. Among his recent books are a collection of stories, *Wanting to Belong* and *Red Landscapes; New and Selected Poems*

Elizabeth Jennings (1926–2001) was born in Lincolnshire and was the only woman poet included in the influential 1956 Movement anthology *New Lines*. Her *New Collected Poems* were published by Carcanet in 2002.

George Jowett lives in Richmond, North Yorkshire. He has published two pamphlets, *Blow by Blow* and *The Old Campaigners*. A life-long fan of boxing, he once sparred with Gerald Suster as a boy.

James Kirkup was born in South Shields in 1918. He has written over forty books, plays and translations including a four volume *Collected Poems* (University of Saltzburg Press). Recent works are: *We of Zipangu* (ARC) poems by Takahashi Mutsuo (bilingual Japanese-English); *A Pilgrim of Hell* (HUB Editions) poems by Belgian "Decadent" Iwan Gilkin (bilingual French-English); and a new collection of poems, *The Authentic Touch* (Bluechrome).

Philip Larkin (1922–85) grew up in Coventry and became the Librarian of Hull University. His poetry collections are *The North Ship, The Less Deceived* and *The Whitsun Weddings* (Faber & Faber).

Michael Laskey founded the Aldeburgh Poetry Festival and edits the poetry magazine *Smiths Knoll*. His collections include *The Tightrope Wedding* and *Permission to Breathe* (Smith/Doorstop Books).

Tom Leonard was born in Glasgow in 1944. His books include *Reports from the Present* and *Access to the Silence* and a biography of the poet James Thomson. He teaches Creative Writing at Glasgow University.

Gwyneth Lewis was born in Cardiff in 1959. She writes in Welsh and in English. Her books include *Zero Gravity* and *Keeping Mum*. She is a recipient of a NESTA award.

Jackie Litherland has lived in Durham City since 1965 and is a member of Durham CCC. She has five poetry collections; her latest being *The Work of the Wind* (Flambard, 2006) and *The Homage* (Iron, 2006), a sequence about the last season of former England cricket captain Nasser Hussain.

John Lucas is the founder of Shoestring Press and author of many critical works, including *The Radical Twenties* (Five Leaves) and seven collections of poetry including *Studying Grosz on the Bus*, winner of the 1990 Aldeburgh poetry prize, and *Flute Music* (Smokestack, 2006*)*.

Roger McGough is a prolific poet, former member of the group The Scaffold and presenter of BBC Radio 4's *Poetry Please* programme. His collections for adults and children include *All the Best* and *Collected Poems* as well as his recent autobiography *Said and Done*. He is a CBE and has been awarded the Freedom of the City of Liverpool.

Ian McMillan was born in Barnsley in 1956. He has worked on a building-site, in a tennis-ball factory and as poet-in-residence at Barnsley FC. A regular broadcaster, he was recently described as the 22nd Most Powerful Person in Radio. His books include *The Invisible Villain* and *Perfect Catch*. He supports Barnsley FC.

Norman MacCaig (1910-96) was born in Edinburgh. He taught for many years in primary schools, later at the universities of Edinburgh and Stirling. He published sixteen collections of poetry, including *The Equal Skies* and *A World of Difference*. His *Collected Poems* were published after his death.

Louis MacNeice (1907-63) was born in Belfast. He taught Classics at the universities of Birmingham and London before joining the BBC as a radio producer. He wrote several plays for stage and radio and many books of poems, including *Autumn Journal* and *Autumn Sequel*. His *Collected Poems* was published after this death.

Jack Mapanje was born in Nyasaland in 1944. He was Head of the Department of English at the University of Malawi when he was arrested and imprisoned for publishing his first book of poems, *Chameleons and Gods*. He was eventually released and came to live in Britain. His most recent book is *The Last of the Sweet Bananas* (Bloodaxe, 2004). He teaches at the School of English, University of Newcastle and is currently working on his prison diaries. He lives in York.

Adrian Mitchell was born in Sussex in 1932. He is a poet, playwright and children's writer and currently 'Shadow Poet Laureate'. His poems are collected in four books — *Greatest Hits, Heart on the Left, Blue Coffee* and *All Shook Up*. His latest book is *The Shadow Knows*. He lives in London and supports Liverpool FC.

Graham Mort was born in Lancashire. He lectures in Creative Writing at Lancaster University and is project leader for the British Council *Crossing Borders* and *Radiophonics* mentoring schemes for African writers. His latest book of poems, *A Night on the Lash,* was published by Seren in 2004. He is currently working on *Visibility*: *New & Selected Poems*.

Andrew Motion was appointed Poet Laureate in 1999. He is Professor of Creative Writing at Royal Holloway, University of London and co-founder of the Poetry Archive. His collections include *The Pleasure Steamers* (Carcanet), *Salt Water* and *Public Property* (Faber & Faber).

Norman Nicholson (1910-87) was born in Millom, in Cumbria and lived all his life in the same house. His books included *A Local Habitation* and *Sea to the West*. He was awarded the Queen's Medal for Poetry.

Sean O'Brien's translation of the *Inferno* was published by Picador in autumn 2006. His next collection of poems, *The Drowned Book*, is to appear in 2007. *Cousin Coat: Selected Poems 1976-2001* appeared in 2002. He is twice winner of the Forward Prize, most recently for *Downriver* (2001). He writes about poetry for the *Sunday Times*, the *TLS* and *The Independent*. He is Professor of Creative Writing at Newcastle University.

Gareth Owen grew up in Ainsdale, Lancashire. He left school at 16 and went to sea before eventually returning to become a teacher. His poetry includes *Salford Road*, which won the Signal Award, *The Fox on the Roundabout*, *Collected Poems* and *The Race*: a verse play about Jesse Owen and the Berlin Olympics which was broadcast by the BBC.

Pascale Petit's last two collections, *The Huntress* (Seren, 2005) and *The Zoo Father* (Seren, 2001, Poetry Book Society Recommendation), were both shortlisted for the TS Eliot Prize and were Books of the Year in the *TLS*. A prize-winning pamphlet *The Wounded Deer – Fourteen poems after Frida Kahlo* (Smith Doorstop) was also published in 2005. In 2004 she was selected as a Next Generation Poet.

David Phillips' *Man in the Long Grass: cricket poems* is published by Iron Press.

Sheenagh Pugh was born in Birmingham in 1950. Her books of poetry include *The Beautiful Lie* and *The Movement of Bodies* (Seren). She currently teaches creative writing at the University of Glamorgan and lives in Cardiff.

Mark Robinson was born in Preston in 1964. He has worked as a vegetarian chef, a literature development officer and a full-time poet. He is currently Executive Director of Arts Council England, North East. His books include *The Horse Burning Park*, *Half a Mind* and a study of poetry readings, *Words Out Loud*. He supports Preston North End.

Neil Rollinson was born in Yorkshire and studied Fine Art at Newcastle before dropping out. After travelling around India and the Far East, he returned to England and wrote *A Spillage of Mercury*. Winner of the National Poetry Competition in 1997, his second collection is *Spanish Fly*.

Michael Rosen was born in London in 1946. He is a prolific and poplar writer of children's books, including *Don't Put Mustard in the Custard* and *Centrally Heated Knickers*. His collections for adults include: *The Skin of Your Back* (Five Leaves) and *Carrying the Elephant*. He lives in London.

Alan Ross (1922-2001) was born in Calcutta. He wrote and edited several books about sport and was for many years cricket correspondent of the *Observer*. He edited the *London Magazine* from 1961-2001. His many books of poems include *The Derelict Day* and the posthumous *Poems*. He represented Oxford University at cricket and squash.

Lawrence Sail has published nine poetry collections, the most recent of which is *Eye-Baby* (Bloodaxe, 2006). He was chairman of the Arvon Foundation from 1990-1994, has directed the Cheltenham Festival of Literature, and received a Cholmondeley Award in 2004.

Peter Sansom is a Creative Writing Fellow at the University of Leeds, and the editor of *The North* and Smith/Doorstop Books. His books include *Writing Poems*, *Everything You've Heard is True* and *Point of Sale*. He lives in Huddersfield.

Siegfried Sassoon (1886-1967) is best known now for the anti-war poetry he wrote during the First World War and the semi-autobiographical novels *Memoirs of a Fox-Hunting Man* and *Memoirs of an Infantry Officer*. He was a keen sportsman and cricket-fan. He wrote many books of poetry, including two volumes of *Collected Poems*.

William Scammell (1939-2000) was born in Hampshire. He left school at 15 and worked in a newspaper office and as a ship's photographer before joining the WEA. His many books included a critical study of Keith Douglas, an edition of Ted Hughes's prose and ten books of his own poetry, including *All Set to Fall Off the Edge of the World* and the posthumously published *Black and White.*

Vernon Scannell was the recipient of the Heinemann Award for Literature in 1960. His many collections include *The Loving Game* (a Poetry Book Society Choice) and *Behind the Lines* (Shoestring Press).

E.J. Scovell (1907-1999) was born in Sheffield. Her books of poetry include *The River Steamer* (Cresset Press), *The Space Between* (Secker & Warburg) and *Collected Poems* (Carcanet).

Chris Searle has worked as a teacher in Canada, Tobago, East London, Mozambique, Grenada and Sheffield. He is a keen cricketer and author of a book about the game, *Pitch of Life.* He writes a weekly jazz column for the *Morning Star.* His most recent book of poems is *Lightning of Your Eyes.*

Charles Sorley (1895-1915) was educated at Marlborough College, where he distinguished himself as a cross-country runner. He volunteered for military service at the beginning of the First World War and rose to the rank of Captain. He was killed at the Battle of Loos. A collection of his poems was published the following year.

Jean Sprackland lives in Southport. Her collections are *Tattoos for Mother's Day* (Spike) and *Hard Water* (Cape) which was short listed for the T.S. Eliot Poetry Prize in 2004.

J.C. Squire (1882-1958) was born in Plymouth. He was the literary editor of the *New Statesman* and later editor of the *London Mercury*. His poems appeared in *Collected Parodies* and the posthumous *Collected Poems*.

Pauline Stainer is an award winning poet and tutor with six collections to her name including *The Wound-dresser's Dream* (1996), which was shortlisted for the Whitbread Poetry Award, *The Honeycomb* (1989), *The Ice-Pilot Speaks* (1994) and *The Lady & The Hare: New & Selected Poems* (2003). She lives in Hadleigh, Suffolk.

Subhadassi was born in Huddersfield, and ordained into the Western Buddhist Order in 1992. Originally a chemistry lecturer, his books include *Sublunary Voodoo* and *peeled*. He lives in London.

George Szirtes came to England as an eight year old refugee after the Hungarian uprising. He has published three collections with Bloodaxe, *The Budapest File, An English Apocalypse* and *Reel* which won the 2004 T.S. Eliot Poetry Prize.

Gael Turnbull (1928–2004) was a doctor by training and a source of inspiration to many British poets during his lifetime. His last major collection was *For Whose Delight* (Mariscat Press).

Gopi Warrier was born in Kerala, India. He is the chairman of a management consulting firm and alternative medical company who has written three collections of poetry, the latest being *Lament of JC* (The Delhi London Poetry Foundation).

Daniel Weissbort co-founded the journal *Modern Poetry in Translation* with Ted Hughes in 1965 and spent nearly thirty years at the University of Iowa, USA as Director of the Translation Workshop. He is the author of several volumes of poetry and over a dozen translations of mainly Russian poets.

Susan Wicks is Director of the Centre for Creative Writing at the University of Kent. She has published two novels, a memoir and four collections of poetry including *Singing Underwater* (Faber) which won the Aldeburgh Poetry Festival Prize, and *The Clever Daughter* which was short listed for both the T.S. Eliot and Forward Prizes. Her new collection, *De-iced*, will be published by Bloodaxe in 2007.

Keith Wilson has worked as a contracted poet at almost every significant sporting event for all the major broadcasters in the UK and Ireland. His publications include *This Is Anfield Calling* and *Irritable Vowel Syndrome*.

P.G. Wodehouse (1881-1975) was a prolific and best-selling comic novelist, creator of Lord Emsworth, Psmith, Mulliner, Bertie Wooster and Jeeves. He also worked as a Hollywood screenwriter and wrote songs for the shows *Anything Goes* and *Show Boat*.

Kit Wright lectured in Canada before working as Education Officer at the Poetry Society and as a Fellow Commoner in Creative Art at Cambridge University. His poetry is collected in *Hoping It Might Be So: Poems 1974-2000* (Leviathan).

Acknowledgements

The editors and publishers gratefully acknowledge permission from the copyright holders to reprint poems in this anthology.

Fleur Adcock: 'Game' is from *Poems 1960-2000* (Bloodaxe, 2000)

Allan Ahlberg: 'Friendly Matches' is from *Friendly Matches* (Viking, 2001)

John Arlott: 'Cricket at Worcester, 1938' and 'To John Berry Hobbs on his Seventieth Birthday' are published by kind permission of the Arlott Estate

Simon Armitage: 'Great Sporting Moments: The Treble' is from *Kid* (Faber and Faber Ltd, 1992)

Mike Barlow: 'Rolling' and 'Offshore with Edward Hopper' are from *Living on the Difference'* (Smith/Doorstop, 2004)

John Betjeman: 'A Subaltern's Love Song', 'Henley Regatta 1902', 'Hunter Trials' and 'Upper Lambourne' are from *John Betjeman: Collected Poems* (John Murray, 1955). Reproduced by permission of John Murray (Publishers)

James Berry: 'Fast Bowler' is from *Hot Earth Cold Earth* (Bloodaxe, 1995)

Jean 'Binta' Breeze: 'on cricket, sex and housework' is from *The Arrival of Brighteye & Other Poems* (Bloodaxe, 2000); 'Song for Lara' is from *On the Edge of an Island* (Bloodaxe, 1997)

Alan Bold: 'The Swimmer' is from *The Poetry of Motion* (Mainstream, 1986), copyright Alan Bold to Alice Bold

Adrian Buckner: 'Cricket at Thrumpton' is from *One Man Queue* (Leafe Press, 2004)

Kevin Cadwallender: 'A Game of Two Halves' was first published in Ian Horn (ed) *Verses United* (Portcullis, 1993)

Kate Clanchy: 'Teams' is from *Slattern*, Chatto & Windus 1995. By permission of the author and Macmillan, London

Brendan Cleary: 'Brian's Fables' is from *The Irish Card* (Bloodaxe, 1993)

Mandy Coe: 'Ten Pin' is from *The Weight of Cows* (Shoestring Press, 2004) and 'Live Match – Big Screen' is from *Pinning the Tail on the Donkey* (Spike, 2000)

Barry Cole: 'Learning to Swim' is from *Ghosts are People Too* (Shoestring Press, 2003)

Stanley Cook: 'Racing Cyclist' was first published in *The Poetry of Motion* (Mainstream, 1986)

Wendy Cope: 'The Cricketing Versions' is from *Serious Concerns* (Faber and Faber Ltd, 1992). Reprinted by permission of PFD on behalf of Wendy Cope © Wendy Cope

David Craig: 'Into Rock' is from *Native Stones* (Secker and Warburg, 1987), 'Life-Line' is from *Against Looting* (Giant Steps, 1987)

Andy Croft: 'Mile 3' and 'Mile 12' are from *Great North* (Iron Press, 2001); 'Methuselah's Losers' is from *Just as Blue* (Flambard, 2001)

Simon Curtis: 'Sports Field, South Manchester' and 'Gloucestershire Alliance, 1985' are from *Reading a River: New and Selected* Poems (Shoestring Press, 2005)

Alan Dent: 'This Sporting Life' is from *Bedtime Story* (Redbeck Press, 1991)

Jeremy Duffield: 'Cross-Country Runners' is printed by permission of the author

David Duncombe: 'Going for Silver' and 'Skittleball Keeper' are from *Joy Rider* (Poetry Monthy Press, 2003)

Helen Dunmore: 'The Sea Skater' is from *Out of the Blue: Poems 1975-2000* (Bloodaxe, 2001)

Douglas Dunn: 'In Ten Seconds' was written for the BBC1 film *Athletes*; 'Runners' is from *The Happier Life*; by permission of Faber and Faber Ltd., 1972

Sue Dymoke: 'Games before Tea' and 'Swimmingly' are from *The New Girls* (Shoestring Press, 2004), 'All in a Game' is printed by permission of the author

U.A. Fanthorpe: 'Hang-gliders in January' is from *Standing To* (Peterloo Poets, 1982)

Vicki Feaver: 'Swimming in January' from *The Handless Maiden* published by Jonathan Cape. Reprinted by permission of The Random House Group Ltd.

Kevin Fegan: extract from 'Racer' commissioned & broadcast by BBC Radio 4 Drama, 2002, and published by Five Leaves

Elaine Feinstein: 'Fishing' from *Collected Poems and Translations* (Carcanet Press Ltd, 2002)

Linda France: 'Polo at Windsor' is from *Storyville* (Bloodaxe, 1997)

Rosie Garner: 'On Football and Killing Chickens' is printed by permission of the author

Pamela Gillilan: 'The Half Mile' is from *All-Steel Traveller: New and Selected Poems* (Bloodaxe, 1994)

Martin Green: 'Ode to Hackney Marshes' is printed by permission of the author

Jane Griffiths: 'The Skater' is from *A Grip on Thin Air* (Bloodaxe, 2000)

Cathy Grindrod: 'Taking Sides' is printed by permission of the author

Mike Harding: 'Daddy Edgar's Pools' is from *Daddy Edgar's Pools* (Peterloo, 1992)

Tony Harrison: 'Divisions' was first published in *From 'The School of Eloquence' and Other Poems* (Rex Collings, 1978), copyright Tony Harrison, *Selected Poems* (Penguin, 1987)

Spike Hawkins: 'The Five to Six Results' is printed by permission of the author

Seamus Heaney: 'The Salmon Fisher to the Salmon' is from *Door into the Dark* (Faber and Faber Ltd, 1969)

Hamish Henderson: 'Heroic Song for the Runners of Cyrene' is from *Elegies for The Dead in Cyrenaica* (John Lehman, 1948)

Selima Hill: 'My Happiest Day' is from *Violet* (Bloodaxe, 1997)

Jane Holland: 'Baize Queens' is from *The Brief History of a Disreputable Woman* (Bloodaxe, 1997)

Ian Horn: 'In the Moonlight a Football' is from *Jazz from the Collieries* (Mudfog Press, 2001)

Michael Horovitz: The excerpt from Michael Horovitz's *The Game* comes from one section of *The Wolverhampton Wanderer: An Epic of Britannia,* first published in 1971 by Latimer New Dimensions

Ted Hughes: 'Football at Slack' was first published in *Remains of Elmet* (Faber and Faber Ltd, 1979); 'Eighty, and Still Fishing for Salmon' was first published in *River* (Faber and Faber Ltd, 1983)

Elizabeth Jennings: 'The Climbers' is from *New Collected Poems* (Carcanet, 2002)

David Jacobs: 'Snooker Players' is from *The Gardens of Onkel Arnold* (Peterloo Poets, 2004)

Mike Jenkins: 'The Pwll Massacre' is from *Red Landscapes: New and Selected Poems* (Seren, 1999)

George Jowett: 'Blow by Blow' is part of a much longer poem from *The Old Campaigners* (Redbeck Press, 2001)

James Kirkup: 'Rugby League Game' is from *Refusal to Conform* (OUP, 1963); 'Synchronised Swimming' is printed by permission of the author

Philip Larkin: 'At Grass' is reprinted from *The Less Deceived* by permission of The Marvell Press, England and Australia

Michael Laskey: 'Sea-Anglers' is from *Thinking of Happiness* (Peterloo, 1991)

Tom Leonard: 'Yon Night' is from *Intimate Voices* (Etruscan Books, 2003)

Gwyneth Lewis: 'A Golf-Course Resurrection' is from *Chaotic Angels* (Bloodaxe, 2005)

Jackie Litherland: 'Bad Light' is from *The Homage* (IRON Press, 2006)

John Lucas: 'An Irregular Ode on the Retirement of Derek Randall, Cricketer' is from *One for the Piano* (Redbeck Press 1997); 'What Holds Them' is from *Flute Music* (Smokestack Books, 2006)

Roger McGough: 'Cousin Caroline', 'Uncle Jed' and 'Uncle Philip' were first published in *Sporting Relations* (Methuen, 1974); '40-love' was first published in *After the Merrymaking* (Cape, 1971)

Ian McMillan: 'Home Support' is from *I Found This Shirt* (Carcanet, 1998), 'The Tennis Ball Poem' is from *How the Hornpipe Failed and Other Poems* (Rivelin Grapheme Press, 1984), 'Three Boring Miles on the Exercise Bike' is from *Dad, the Donkey's on Fire* (Carcanet, 1994)

Norman MacCaig: 'Highland Games' was first published in *Equal Skies* (Chatto and Windus, 1980) and is reproduced by permission of Polygon, an imprint of Birlinn Ltd.

Louis MacNeice: 'The Cyclist' is from *Collected Poems* (Faber, 1966)

Jack Mapanje: 'Skipping Without Ropes' is from *The Last of the Sweet Bananas* (Bloodaxe, 2004)

Adrian Mitchell: 'By the Waters of Liverpool' is from *Blue Coffee* (Bloodaxe, 1996)

Graham Mort: 'Climbing at Heptonstall Quarry' is from *Sky Burial* (Dangaroo Press, 1989); 'Climbing with a Dead Man' is from *Snow from the North* (Dangaroo Press, 1992)

Andrew Motion: 'A Severe Absence of Fish' is from *Salt Water* (Faber, 1997). Reprinted by permission of PFD on behalf of Andrew Motion, © Andrew Motion

Norman Nicholson: 'The Field' is from *Collected Poems* (Faber and Faber, 1994)

Sean O'Brien: 'Cantona' is from *Ghost Train* (Oxford, 1995); 'Football! Football! Football!' and 'Dignified' are from *Downriver* (Picador, 2001)

Gareth Owen: 'Ping-Pong' ©1971 by Gareth Owen, first published in *Wordscapes*, reprinted by permission of Rogers, Coleridge & White Ltd.

Pascale Petit: 'Portrait of My Brother as an Endurance Runner' is from *The Huntress* (Seren, 2005)

David Phillips: 'Pyjama Pickle' is from *Man in the Long Grass* (Iron, 2001)

Sheenagh Pugh: 'Mozart Playing Billiards' is from *Sing for the Taxman* (Seren, 1993)

Mark Robinson: 'Rio de Juninho' is from *Gaps Between Hills* (Scratch, 1996)

Neil Rollinson: 'Deep-Third-Man', 'The Penalty' and 'The Semis' are from *Spanish Fly* published by Jonathan Cape. Reprinted by permission of The Random House Group Ltd.

Michael Rosen: 'Unfair' is from *Quick, Let's Get Out of Here* (Andre Deutsch, 1983)

Alan Ross: 'Cricket at Brighton' is from *The Poetry of Motion* (Mainstream, 1986)

Lawrence Sail: 'Snooker Players' and 'Fives Courts' are from *Out of Land: New & Selected Poems* (Bloodaxe, 1992)

Peter Sansom: 'If You Can't Finish, You're Buried' is from *Everything You've Heard is True* (Carcanet, 1990)

Siegfried Sassoon: 'The Blues at Lords' is from *Collected Poems* (Faber, 1937). Copyright Siegfried Sassoon by kind permission of the Estate of George Sassoon

William Scammell: 'Arms and the Court', 'Golden Dawn', 'John McEnroe' and 'The Tennis Court Oath' are from *The Game: Tennis Poems* (Peterloo, 1992) and are included here by permission of his wife, Jan Scammell, copyright Estate of William Scammell

Vernon Scannell: the extract from 'First Fight' and 'Mastering the Craft' from *Mastering the Craft* (Elsevier, 1970) are published by permission of the author

E.J. Scovell: 'The Boy Fishing' is from *Collected Poems* (Carcanet Press Limited, 1988)

Chris Searle: 'Balthazar's Poem' is from *Common Ground* (Artery, 1983)

Charles Sorley: 'The Song of the Ungirt Runners' was first published in *Marlborough and other Poems* (CUP, 1916)

Jean Sprackland: 'Synchronised Drowning' is from *Hard Water* published by Jonathan Cape. Reprinted by permission of The Random House Group Ltd.

J.C. Squire: 'The Rugger Match' is from *Collected Poems* (Macmillan, 1959)

Pauline Stainer: 'The Bowls Match' is from *The Lady & the Hare* (Bloodaxe, 2003)

Subhadassi: 'Fishing' is from *peeled* (Arc, 2004)

George Szirtes: 'Preston North End' is from *An English Apocalypse* (Bloodaxe, 2001)

Gael Turnbull: 'A Racing Walker' from *For Whose Delight* (Mariscat Press, 1995) is reprinted by kind permission of Jill Turnbull

225